Hey, can I get that recipe?

THIS COOKBOOK BELONGS TO:

_____

_____

Cheri Renee & kat Tegs designs

INTRODUCTION

Hello fellow home cooks and welcome to my new cookbook! My name is Cheri and I am so excited to share my recipes with you, along with some home cook tips and tricks.

What do you do when you taste something yummy, or see a delicious meal posted on a friend's social media page?! Well, you ask "Hey, Can I get that recipe?", of course.

So I wanted to share with you some of my recipes worthy of asking that question!

I was a second grade teacher for many years, and always had a passion for cooking (or maybe more a passion for eating, so I had to learn to cook). I am 100% self taught, and I know the struggle of making dinner after a long day of working. Over the years I discovered so many tips and tricks to put dinner on the table for my family without completely stressing myself out.

I started my first food blog where I share my recipes online at CooksWellWithOthers.com. I started writing about what I made for my family, which included a few easy dinners and side dishes that I could make during the week. And a few appetizers and fun snacky stuff that I would spend a little more time on the weekends.

And once I stopped teaching to focus on cooking and recipe sharing full time, I was able to start a second food blog IfYouGiveAGirlAGrill.com. This website is about all things outdoor cooking including griddle recipes, grilling, and using my smoker and pellet grill to create fantastic food. My first cookbook was actually a Traeger Grill and Smoker Cookbook for Beginners (available on Amazon!).

Some of the recipes in this book are adapted from a few of my favorite recipes on my websites, but they are all in one place for your convenience.

Feel free to check out my websites often because I am always posting new recipes!

COOKBOOK CHAPTERS

The chapters in my book are a little out of the box and not traditional when it comes to cookbooks. But I really thought long and hard about what home cooks truly want and need in a cookbook. And that's how I decided what to include.

Home cooks are SOOOO much different than the chefs we see on TV, and home cooking is truly a whirlwind of difference compared to restaurant cooking. I mean, not many people look forward to cooking dinner. It's more of a chore for some of us than a passion or a job, like a chef.

Part of the battle is simply coming up with WHAT to make. What to make for dinner, and then there's holidays and parties that present another level of WHAT to bring.

Hopefully I can be of assistance with these wonderings of what to bring and make. AND give you some helpful home cook hacks to make your life a little easier.

That's why you'll find TWO chapters for each of the following, appetizers, side dishes, and dinner.

Because, well, there are two kinds of each... let me explain 🙂

For appetizers, there are those that you make at home and serve right away to your family or maybe a few friends that are over. Think game day snacks or a family movie night in. And then there are appetizers that are expected to feed a crowd at a gathering or party. Not the same, am I right?! But we find ourselves having a need for both types.

Side dishes are the same. We need a few easy side dishes to serve about 4 to 6 people at dinner... and these need to be SUPER easy because I don't know about you, but if I am making dinner I really don't want to fuss over a side dish. And then there are side dishes that you bring to holidays, large family dinners, and celebrations. They need to travel well in addition to serving many people.

And then there are two dinner categories as well... easy meals that I can whip up in no time after working all day that my family will actually eat. And then there are extra special weekend dinners when you have more time, meals to serve to guests or company, and dinners to send over family and friends who are maybe sick or need some extra love in the form of food.

The other two chapters in this cookbook are breakfast/ brunch items and desserts. No need to split those, but remember that the breakfast recipes can ALWAYS be served as dinner... breakfast for dinner is very popular at our house!

RECIPE FEATURES

Each recipe has a bonus section of one of the following...

Helpful Hints- If there's something helpful I can offer you about the recipe, you better believe I will! That's where you'll find some of my tips and tricks.

Home Cook Hacks- If there's a way to simplify a recipe or a hack I have found to make the recipe easier, I have included those as well.

Recipe Variations- If I wrote a recipe, but there are flavor variations, or a way to create a few different versions of the same recipe, I've got ya covered. So some of these are actually 2 to 4 recipes in one!

Cooking Variations- If you can cook the recipe in the air fryer or slow cooker, or even on the grill or griddle I have those instructions included for you.

TIME SAVING TRICKS

Use these time savers if you are really wanting to get dinner on the table quickly...

Garlic- Many of these recipes call for garlic. Personally I despise peeling fresh garlic, so I buy the already peeled garlic that keeps fresh in the fridge. Then I mince a few cloves when cooking. You could take this one step further and buy garlic paste in the tube. It's in the produce section of the store next to the fresh herbs. I find the jar of minced garlic can make food bitter, so that's why I don't prefer to use it.

Onions- If you are not a fan of chopping onions, either due to the fact that they make you cry or just the few minutes it takes to peel and chop them, I've got a trick! Buy the frozen chopped onions that come in a bag. Then use about a cup of those for any recipe that calls for a diced onion.

Foil Pans- I'm not here to give environmental advice, only cooking hacks... but friends, use the disposable foil pans if it will relieve some stress! Especially when bringing dishes to a party or gathering you don't have to worry about bringing it back home. Easy cleanup is our friend 🙂

Marinating- Kind of the same concept as the foil pans, use gallon size plastic bags when marinating. Throw everything in the bag, massage until it's combined, and throw in the fridge. Mess free marinating is pretty awesome. And while we are talking about marinating... do this the night before, especially on busy weeknight. Come home from work, most of the work is done already so making dinner is a cinch.

MEAL PLANNING

It's unrealistic to think you'll make a home cooked meal every single night of the week. And if you do, please teach me your ways!

When I plan meals for the week, I pick 3 to 4 dinners. And usually something fun and snacky on the weekends. We usually have a leftover night one day a week, where basically everyone just makes their own from what's leftover in the fridge or a good old fashioned turkey sandwich works too.

Most of the dinner recipes feed 4 to 6 people, so we do have quite a bit leftover. So even if you don't think your family will eat it all, nothing will go to waste. Cooking once and eating twice is my version of work smarter, not harder.

We either eat out or do pizza night once or twice a week too, because we are only human and it's quite a treat to take a break from cooking.

Personally I love to cook, but even I need a break so I don't get burnt out. Give yourself some grace, relax and order the dang food. Just pat yourself on the back for the meals you DID cook :)

CHAPTER ONE

Breakfast & Brunch

IN MY WORLD, BREAKFAST ISN'T JUST FOR THE MORNING. WE ARE HUGE FANS OF BREAKFAST-FOR-DINNER, SO ALL OF THESE RECIPES CAN BE MADE ANY TIME OF THE DAY.

THESE RECIPES RANGE FROM HOLIDAY-WORTHY CASSEROLES TO SIMPLE, FAMILY STYLE DISHES. SOME ARE EVEN GREAT TO MAKE AHEAD AND WARM UP FOR A BUSY BREAKFAST-ON-THE-GO.

Breakfast Enchiladas

This is a great make-ahead dish! It can be made the night before, stored in the fridge, and baked in the morning. Or earlier in the day to have a great breakfast-for-dinner.

15	60	75	6-8
PREP	COOK	TOTAL	SERVINGS

Ingredients

1 pound ground breakfast sausage

1 onion (diced)

Kosher salt, pepper

1 10 ounce can enchilada sauce (red or green)

6 to 8 taco size soft tortillas (corn or flour)

3 cups shredded cheese of choice

6 eggs

¾ cup milk

Optional: sour cream, salsa, hot sauce

Helpful Hints

Warming the tortillas before rolling will help prevent them from breaking, especially if using corn tortillas.

Directions

1. Set a skillet over medium heat and add the sausage. Cook for 4 to 5 minutes, breaking the sausage apart with a spatula as it cooks.

2. Add the diced onion to the skillet with the sausage, add kosher salt and pepper. Cook 4 to 5 minutes stirring a few times.

3. Add half of the can of green enchilada sauce and let it cook a few more minutes.

4. Allow the sausage mixture to cool slightly. Put a few spoonfuls of the filling down the center of each tortilla with some cheese. Leave about a cup of cheese to sprinkle over top later.

5. Roll them up (leaving ends open) and place them seam side down in a greased 9×13 baking dish. If you have extra filling just put right on top of the enchiladas.

6. Crack the eggs in a bowl, add the milk, the remaining green enchilada sauce, and add some kosher salt and pepper. Whisk together. Pour this mixture over top of the enchiladas. Cover and put in the fridge for at least 4 hours or overnight.

7. Uncover and bake in a 350 degree oven for 30 to 40 minutes. Add the remaining cheese and bake an additional 10 to 12 minutes or until the cheese is melted and the eggs are set and fully cooked.

8. Serve with optional toppings such as sour cream, salsa, and/or hot sauce.

Breakfast Roll Ups

A quick and easy breakfast or brunch that my kids love.
Gotta love anything wrapped in crescent rolls,
little individual bundles of yumminess!

10	15	25	8
PREP	COOK	TOTAL	SERVINGS

Ingredients

3 eggs

2 tablespoons milk

Kosher salt, pepper

2 tablespoons butter

1 tube crescent rolls

8 cooked sausage links

4 slices colby jack cheese
(cut in half)

1 tablespoon pure maple syrup

Cooking Variations

These can also be cooked in your air fryer! Set the air fryer to 370 degrees for 7 to 9 minutes.

Directions

1. Crack the eggs in a bowl and add the milk, kosher salt, and pepper. Beat the eggs with a fork.

2. Set a small skillet over medium low heat and add 1 tablespoon of the butter. Add the eggs and cook for 3 to 4 minutes, scrambling as they cook with a spatula.

3. Separate the triangle pieces of crescent roll dough and lay them flat.

4. Add some scrambled eggs to each, then a cooked sausage link and half slice of cheese. Roll each one up and place on a lined baking sheet.

5. Bake in a 375 degree oven for 13 to 16 minutes. Melt the remaining tablespoon of butter and mix together with the maple syrup. Brush this over the roll ups during the last few minutes of cooking.

Chorizo Breakfast Burritos

These breakfast burritos are awesome with a little spicy kick from the chorizo and pepper jack cheese. I love to add a drizzle of maple syrup for a sweet and spicy flavor combo!

15	12	27	12
PREP	COOK	TOTAL	SERVINGS

Ingredients

1 pound ground chorizo sausage

8 eggs

½ cup milk

Kosher salt, pepper

2 tablespoons butter

12 soft taco size flour tortillas

12 slices pepper jack cheese

Optional: maple syrup, hot sauce

Home Cook Hacks

Roll the individual burritos in foil or plastic wrap and freeze them for a quick breakfast on the go. Just reheat in the microwave for a minute or two and enjoy!

If you sear the burritos, this can be done on the griddle or flat top grill.

Directions

1. If your chorizo came in links with a casing, cut down the center of each sausage link and remove the casing.

2. Crack the eggs in a bowl and add the milk, kosher salt, and pepper. Beat with a fork until combined.

3. Set a large skillet over medium heat and add the chorizo sausage. Cook for 4 to 5 minutes, breaking it apart with a spatula. Remove the sausage, wipe the skillet clean, and set it back on the stove still over medium heat.

4. Add the butter and eggs. Scramble the eggs as they cook for 3 to 5 minutes. Remove the eggs and let them cool before making the burritos.

5. To assemble each burrito, cut a slice of pepper jack cheese in half and place in the center of each tortilla. Add some egg, sausage, a drizzle of maple syrup and/ or hot sauce if using. Fold the sides in and tightly roll into a burrito.

6. Optional: Cook the burritos in the skillet over medium heat with a little more butter for a minute or two per side to toast and crisp the tortillas. This will need to be done in a few smaller batches.

Frosted Flake French Toast

This sweet breakfast treat brings a crispy crunch factor to traditional french toast. A good, quality bread makes a difference. I love the thick cut brioche bread the best!

10	10	20	8
PREP	COOK	TOTAL	SERVINGS

Ingredients

4 cups Frosted Flake cereal

4 eggs

½ cup milk

1 teaspoon vanilla extract

1 teaspoon sugar

3 tablespoons butter

8 slices bread

Maple syrup

Home Cook Hacks

If you have flavored coffee creamer, use it in place of the milk. It will add some extra sweetness and flavor, and make a more decadent french toast.

These can also be cooked all at once on a griddle or flat tip grill.

Directions

1. Put the Frosted Flake cereal in a gallon size plastic bag. Use a rolling pin or cup to crush them. Put the crushed cereal in a bowl.

2. Crack the eggs in a separate bowl and add the milk, vanilla, and sugar. Beat with a fork.

3. Set a large skillet over medium low heat. Once hot add some of the butter and spread evenly.

4. Dip a few slices of bread in the egg mixture and then into the Frosted Flakes. Place in the skillet and cook for 2 to 3 minutes per side. Repeat with the remaining bread.

5. Serve with maple syrup.

Goetta Bacon Breakfast Sliders

Little breakfast sandwiches with crispy goetta and bacon, melty cheesy goodness, and topped with maple butter for some added sweetness.

10	30	40	12
PREP	COOK	TOTAL	SERVINGS

Ingredients

1 pound goetta

Olive oil

1 12 pack slider rolls

10 to 12 slices cooked bacon

8 slices provolone cheese

2 tablespoons melted butter

2 tablespoons pure maple syrup

Cooking Variations

If you can't find goetta, use cooked breakfast sausage patties instead. Also, feel free to add some scrambled eggs to the sliders. Mix it up with different cheeses like cheddar, swiss, or pepper jack.

Directions

1. Cut the goetta into slices. Set a skillet over medium heat and add a little olive oil. Cook the goetta slices, a few at a time, 4 to 5 minutes per side. Repeat with the remaining goetta slices.

Note: Goetta is very delicate, so allow the full 4 to 5 minutes before flipping, flipping too early can cause it to fall apart.

2. Slice the slider rolls in half if needed and place on a baking sheet (I used King's Hawaiian Sweet Rolls and used a serrated bread knife to slice them in half).

3. Arrange the goetta slices on the bottom half of the slider buns, top with the cooked bacon, and cheese slices (overlapping slightly).

4. Put the top half of the slider buns on and press slightly. Mix together the melted butter and syrup, brush on the top half of the buns.

5. Bake the sliders in a 350 degree oven for 18 to 20 minutes or until the cheese is melted.

Sausage Gravy with Biscuits

This classic breakfast dish is so easy to make at home!
I used store bought biscuits to save some time, and included
some flavor variations to mix this recipe up in a few ways.

10	20	30	4
PREP	COOK	TOTAL	SERVINGS

Ingredients

1 tablespoon olive oil

1 pound country breakfast sausage

1 onion (diced)

Kosher salt, pepper,
   crushed red pepper flakes

¼ cup flour

2½ cups whole milk

8 count package/tube jumbo biscuits

Recipe Variations

Use goetta or chorizo sausage in place of the breakfast sausage. Also add a 4 ounce can of green chiles or jalapenos to add some heat. For a creamy, cheesy version stir in a cup of shredded cheese of choice during the last few minutes of cooking.

Directions

1. Set a large skillet over medium heat, add the olive oil, sausage, diced onion, kosher salt, pepper, and crushed red pepper flakes. Cook 7 to 9 minutes, stirring a few times and breaking the sausage apart with a spatula.

2. Sprinkle some of the flour, stir until combined. Add a little more flour and stir. Then add the rest of the flour and stir for another 2 to 3 minutes.

3. Add the milk, more kosher salt and pepper and bring to a boil. Once boiling, reduce the heat to low and stir occasionally for about 10 to 12 minutes.

4. Bake the biscuits according to the package directions. Serve the sausage gravy over the cooked biscuits.

Sausage & Waffle Breakfast Casserole

This is a fabulous dish to serve for a holiday or celebration. Or it makes for one of our favorite breakfast-for-dinner meals! And if you like things on the sweeter side, an extra drizzle of maple syrup does the trick.

10	45	55	8
PREP	COOK	TOTAL	SERVINGS

Ingredients

1 pound breakfast sausage

8 frozen toaster waffles

1½ cups shredded cheddar cheese

8 eggs

1¼ cups milk

½ pure maple syrup

Recipe Variations

You could easily substitute a pound of diced ham for the sausage, and even play around with different cheeses like Swiss or Colby Jack. Or use cooked, seasoned chicken in place of the sausage for a fun chicken and waffle casserole

Directions

1. In a skillet over medium heat, cook the breakfast sausage for 5 to 8 minutes until fully cooked.

2. Toast the waffles and then cut into cubes. Place into a greased 9×13 baking dish (or foil pan for easy clean up). Add the cooked sausage and cheese and toss together until evenly combined.

3. In a bowl beat the eggs, milk, and maple syrup together with a whisk or fork. Pour over top the waffles, sausage and cheese. Press the waffles slightly into the egg mixture.

4. Bake in a 375 degree oven for 45 to 50 minutes. Serve with extra maple syrup on the side if desired.

Zucchini Muffins with Brown Sugar Glaze

Normally I don't do vegetables for breakfast,
but for these delicious muffins I make an exception.
A great way to use garden fresh zucchini!

10	25	35	24
PREP	COOK	TOTAL	SERVINGS

Ingredients

3 cups all purpose flour

2 cups sugar

2 teaspoons baking soda

1 teaspoon ground cinnamon

1 teaspoon nutmeg

1 teaspoon kosher salt

1 cup vegetable oil

3 eggs

½ cup milk

1 teaspoon vanilla extract

3 cups grated zucchini

¼ cup melted butter

¼ cup brown sugar

Nonstick cooking spray

Directions

1. Add flour, sugar, baking soda, cinnamon, nutmeg, and kosher salt to a bowl and stir until evenly mixed.

2. In a separate bowl add the oil and eggs. Beat with a hand mixer on medium speed for 1 minute.

3. Add the milk, vanilla, and a cup of the dry ingredients and beat on medium speed. Continue to add more dry ingredients and beat until all of the dry ingredients are added and batter is smooth, be careful not to overmix.

4. Stir in the grated zucchini.

Recipe Variations

You can easily add some chocolate chips to the batter or mix in some chopped pecans if desired.

5. Scoop
the batter
into muffin
tins (24 total)
either sprayed
with nonstick
spray or
use paper
muffin liners.

6. Bake in a
350 degree
oven for
18 to 22 minutes.

7. Mix together
the melted butter
and brown sugar.
Brush the over the muffins
and bake for 4 to 5 more minutes.

8. Let cool before serving.

CHAPTER TWO

Stay at Home Snacks & Appetizers

IN MY OPINION, APPETIZERS AND SNACKS COME
IN TWO DISTINCT CATEGORIES… THE ONES YOU
MAKE AND ENJOY AT HOME WITH A SMALL
GROUP. AND THEN THERE'S THE ONES
YOU MAKE FOR A CROWD.

THIS CHAPTER IS FILLED WITH
THE FIRST CATEGORY.

Beer Brined Chicken Wings

Wings are SO easy to make and enjoy at home, and these are on the healthier side because they aren't deep fried. Sauce and seasoning options are endless! With this basic recipe you can turn your wings into any flavor you desire... BBQ, buffalo, explore the different store bought seasonings and sauces that are available.

10	45	55	5 lbs
PREP	COOK	TOTAL	SERVINGS

Ingredients

5 pounds jumbo split chicken wings

2 12 ounces bottles or cans of your favorite beer

1 cup water

¼ cup kosher salt

¼ cup brown sugar

4 tablespoons favorite seasoning blend of choice (BBQ, Caribbean Jerk, all purpose blend, etc.)

Optional: wing sauce of choice, ranch dressing

Cooking Variations

These wings can also be cooked in a smoker or pellet grill set to 250 degrees for two and a half hours, flipping them halfway through. Or in the air fryer set to 380 degrees for 20 to 25 minutes, flipping halfway through.

Directions

1. Put the jumbo split wings into a gallon size plastic bag. Add the beer, water, salt, brown sugar, and 2 tablespoons of your seasoning blend. Massage the bag until evenly mixed and place in the fridge 24 hours, place in a bowl in case of a leak.

2. Remove the chicken wings, discard the brine. Pat the wings dry with paper towels. Sprinkle with the remaining 2 tablespoons of your seasoning.

3. Place wings on a lined baking sheet and put in a 400 degree oven for 45 to 50 minutes, flip them halfway through. Make sure they are at an internal temperature of 165 degrees.

4. Serve with any sauce of choice if desired and with ranch dressing for dipping.

Buffalo Chicken Roll Ups

Something cheesy and buffalo-y is always
a great combo for an at home appetizer!

5	15	20	6
PREP	COOK	TOTAL	SERVINGS

Ingredients

1 tube refrigerated pizza crust
1 cup cooked, shredded chicken (p. 87)
1 cup buffalo wing sauce
1½ cups shredded cheddar cheese
½ cup blue cheese crumbles (**optional**)
Optional: Ranch dressing for dipping

Recipe Variations

You could use leftover pulled
pork and BBQ sauce in place of
the chicken and buffalo sauce
for this recipe. Or make pizza roll
ups using pepperoni, pizza sauce
or pesto, and mozzarella!

Directions

1. Roll your pizza dough
flat and evenly distribute
the chicken, half of the
buffalo wing sauce,
cheddar cheese, and blue
cheese (if using).

2. Tightly roll it up and cut
into 12 slices. Place roll
ups on a baking sheet.
Top each with the extra
buffalo sauce.

3. Bake in a 425 degree
oven for 10 to 15
minutes, until cooked
through and golden brown
and serve with ranch
dressing for dipping.

Cheesy Garlic Bombs

Carbs are always welcome in our house, especially when cheese is involved! These are a great appetizer or as a side dish served with spaghetti, steak, or lasagna.

10	15	25	8
PREP	COOK	TOTAL	SERVINGS

Ingredients

1 package crescent rolls

8 cubes mozzarella cheese (about an inch in size)

3 tablespoons melted butter

1 teaspoon garlic powder

1 teaspoon Italian seasoning

Kosher salt, pepper

Pizza sauce

Cooking Variations

Cook these garlic bombs in the air fryer instead of the oven if preferred. Place them in the air fryer basket, set it to 380 degrees for 5 to 6 minutes. Brush the garlic butter over top and air fry for another 2 to 3 minutes.

Directions

1. Separate the crescent rolls into 8 triangles and lay them flat.

2. Put a cube of cheese in the center of each and wrap the crescent dough around the cheese, sealing all edges closed.

3. Place on a baking sheet and bake in a 375 degree oven for 12 to 14 minutes.

4. Mix together the melted butter, garlic powder, Italian seasoning, kosher salt, and pepper. Brush the butter on them and bake for another 2 to 3 minutes. Serve with pizza sauce for dipping.

Fried Bang Bang Shrimp

My favorite restaurant appetizer is bang bang (or sometimes called boom boom) shrimp. This sweet and spicy sauce is SO easy to make at home and deep frying in a saucepan doesn't have to be scary. You got this!

10	10	20	4
PREP	COOK	TOTAL	SERVINGS

Ingredients

1 pound jumbo shrimp
   (peeled and deveined)
1 cup buttermilk
1 cup cornstarch
Vegetable oil (enough to fill a small
   saucepan 2 to 3 inches deep)
½ cup mayo
½ cup sweet Thai chili sauce
2 to 3 tablespoons sriracha

Helpful Hints

Use a back burner on the stove, especially if kids are around. If the oil gets too hot, just remove from the heat for a few minutes and fry the shrimp when the oil is at 350 degrees. You can easily turn this appetizer into a meal and serve over cooked Jasmine rice.

Directions

1. Put the shrimp in a bowl with the buttermilk. Put the cornstarch in a separate bowl. Fill a saucepan with vegetable oil 2 to 3 inches deep over medium heat.

2. While the oil heats up, put the mayo, sweet chili sauce, and sriracha in a bowl and mix until combined. Set another plate out with paper towels to put the shrimp after they are fried.

3. Once the oil reaches 350 degrees put 5 to 6 shrimp in the cornstarch and toss to coat them. Then gently place them in the oil. Fry for 2 to 3 minutes and put them on the plate lined with paper towels. Repeat frying the remaining shrimp.

4. Toss the shrimp with the bang bang sauce to coat and serve right away.

Jalapeño Popper Stuffed Mushrooms

A slightly spicy and cheesy game day snack or party appetizer to enjoy at home! An easy to make filling turns regular stuffed mushrooms into something extraordinary.

10	20	30	15
PREP	COOK	TOTAL	SERVINGS

Ingredients

8 ounces cream cheese
(at room temperature)
8 slices bacon
(cooked and crumbled)
1 cup shredded cheddar cheese
2 to 3 jalapenos (minced,
seeds and stems removed)
Kosher salt, pepper
1 pound baby portobello mushrooms

Directions

1. Mix together the cream cheese, bacon crumbles, shredded cheese, jalapenos, kosher salt, and pepper in a bowl.

2. Remove the stems from the mushrooms and put the cream cheese mixture in each mushroom.

3. Place the stuffed mushrooms on a baking sheet and place in a 400 degree oven for 18 to 22 minutes.

Cooking Variations

You can easily use your air fryer to make both the bacon and the mushrooms! Lay the bacon flat in the air fryer basket, set the air fryer to 400 degrees for 10 minutes. Once the mushrooms are stuffed, put them in the air fryer basket at 400 degrees for 8 to 10 minutes. Depending on your air fryer the bacon and mushrooms may need to be done in two smaller batches.

Meatball Sub Bites

These are like mini meatball subs made in a muffin tin. And, like most of these recipes, they are super easy to make because we are using frozen meatballs!

10	15	25	12
PREP	COOK	TOTAL	SERVINGS

Ingredients

1 package crescent rolls

Nonstick cooking spray

1½ cups shredded mozzarella cheese

12 frozen meatballs (thawed)

1 cup pizza sauce

Garlic powder, Italian seasoning

Recipe Variations

Use the same crescent cups to make chili cheese dog bites! Use cheddar cheese in place of the mozzarella, and use 3 hot dogs cut into 4 pieces each in place of the meatballs. And 1 to 1½ cups of canned or leftover homemade chili in place of the pizza sauce. No need to use the Italian seasoning or garlic powder for this version.

Directions

1. Lay the crescent roll flat and pinch the seams together, Use a pizza cutter to cut into 12 equal pieces.

2. Spray a muffin tin with nonstick cooking spray and place each crescent roll piece in the muffin tins. Pinch the edges together to form a cup.

3. Put some of the cheese down first in each crescent cup. Then place a meatball in each. Spoon the pizza sauce over each meatball and top with remaining cheese.

4. Sprinkle some garlic powder and Italian seasoning over each bite and place in a 375 degree oven for 14 to 16 minutes.

The Crispiest Baked Chicken Wings

So, yes... this is the second wing recipe for this chapter.
BUT, this recipe has a few secret tips for the crispiest skin!

10	45	55	4 lbs
PREP	COOK	TOTAL	SERVINGS

Ingredients

4 pounds jumbo split chicken wings

2 to 3 tablespoons seasoning blend of choice (Cajun, Old Bay, or BBQ)

1 tablespoon baking powder

Wing sauce of choice

Home Cook Hacks

Whenever I toss something in sauce I like to put the sauce in a plastic container with a lid. Put the chicken wings into the container, secure the lid, and toss to make the wings evenly coated in a very simple way.

Directions

1. Pat the chicken wings dry with paper towels.

2. Mix together the seasoning and the baking powder. Rub this on all sides of the dry chicken wings.

3. Place a wire baking rack over a lined baking sheet. Put the wings on the wire baking rack. Bake in a 475 degree oven for 45 to 50 minutes, flip the wings half way through.

4. Toss with your favorite chicken wing sauce before serving.

Tomato Pesto Puffed Pastries

Store bought puff pastry can be a home cook's best friend. So many ways to use this magical ingredient that makes you feel like a fancy chef and a star in your very own kitchen.

10	20	30	9
PREP	COOK	TOTAL	SERVINGS

Ingredients

1 sheet puff pastry
   (2 come in a pack, I just used one)

1 to 2 tablespoons flour

4 ounces pesto

1 cup cherry or grape tomatoes

6 to 8 ounces fresh mozzarella cheese

Kosher salt, pepper

Balsamic glaze
   (vinegar aisle of grocery store)

Recipe Variations

Add some cooked, shredded chicken or cooked steak slices to this version in place of the tomatoes if desired. Or swap out the mozzarella cheese for some goat cheese. You could really get creative and make mini puff pastry pizzas with pizza sauce and any toppings your heart desires.

Directions

1. Thaw the puff pastry according to package directions. Sprinkle the flour on a flat surface and lay the puff pastry sheet flat. Roll the sheet slightly thinner with a rolling pin. Use a pizza cutter to cut into 9 squares.

2. Poke the center of each square several times with a fork, leaving the outer edge with no fork marks. Careful not to poke through the puff pastry. Place the squares on a baking sheet.

3. Spread the pesto on each puff pastry square. Cut the tomatoes in half and place them over the pesto. Cut the fresh mozzarella into smaller cubes and arrange them beside the tomatoes. Sprinkle with kosher salt and pepper.

4. Bake in a 400 degree oven for 18 to 20 minutes. Drizzle the balsamic glaze over top and serve right away.

CHAPTER THREE

Party & Holiday Appetizers

THERE'S A PARTY, HOLIDAY CELEBRATION, SUMMER PICNIC... WHATEVER THE FUN OCCASION, YOUR JOY CAN SLOWLY TURN INTO WORRY ABOUT WHAT IN THE WORLD TO BRING.

IT'S GOTTA TRAVEL WELL, FEED A CROWD, SIMPLE ENOUGH INGREDIENTS SO EVERYONE WILL LOVE IT, BUT WITH A CERTAIN WOW FACTOR... YOU KNOW, SO EVERYONE ASKS

"HEY, CAN I GET THAT RECIPE?".

WELL FRIENDS, THIS CHAPTER IS DEDICATED TO ALL RECIPES THAT FIT THIS DESCRIPTION.

BLT Cresent Pizza

The inspiration behind this cold appetizer is the common veggie pizza. But this one has yummy BLT toppings! This recipe does make a TON, you can cut it in half if you'd like.

10	20	30	15
PREP	COOK	TOTAL	SERVINGS

Ingredients

1 to 1½ pounds bacon
  (depending on preference)
Nonstick cooking spray
3 tubes crescent rolls
2 8 ounce blocks cream cheese
  (at room temperature)
1 cup mayo
1 packet dry ranch seasoning
3 cups shredded lettuce
3 cups shredded cheddar cheese
3 to 4 tomatoes (diced)
Kosher salt, pepper

Directions

1. Set a large skillet over medium heat. Use kitchen scissors to cut the bacon into bite size pieces right into the skillet. Cook for 7 to 9 minutes, stirring a few times. Remove the bacon and place on a plate lined with paper towels.

2. Spray a large baking sheet or two smaller baking sheets with nonstick spray. Unroll the crescent dough flat on the baking sheet(s). Press the seams on the crescent dough together and use a fork to poke the dough several times all over.

Helpful Hints

Press down on the toppings slightly and put in the fridge for at least an hour before cutting and serving. I recommend using a pizza cutter to cut these. Any leftover toppings that come off while cutting can just be sprinkled back on top after cutting.

3. Bake the dough in a 375 degree oven for 10 to 12 minutes and let cool.

4. Mix the cream cheese, mayo, and dry ranch seasoning together in a bowl with a hand mixer for a minute. Spread this evenly over the cooked and cooled crescent dough.

5. Evenly spread the lettuce and cheese over top. Put the diced tomatoes on a plate lined with paper towels for a minute or two to soak up any extra liquid, season them with kosher salt and pepper. Sprinkle the tomatoes and cooked bacon crumbles over top.

Cheesy Jalapeño Popper Dip

This is a great appetizer that is amazing served warm or at room temperature. Always a hit at every party or celebration!

10	40	50	10
PREP	COOK	TOTAL	SERVINGS

Ingredients

Nonstick cooking spray

2 8 ounce blocks cream cheese

3 to 4 jalapeno peppers
(seeds removed and diced)

2 cups shredded cheddar or
Colby Jack cheese

1 cup mayonaise

3 green onions (sliced)

2½ tablespoons dry ranch seasoning

Optional: more cheese and green onions over top before serving, tortilla chips or Fritos Scoops for dipping

Directions

1. Spray a large cast iron skillet or casserole dish with nonstick spray. Put all ingredients into the skillet or casserole dish. No need to stir yet.

2. Place in a 300 degree oven for 20 minutes. Stir until evenly combined and bake for another 20 minutes.

3. Serve with more cheese and green onions over top if desired and with tortilla chips or Fritos Scoops for dipping.

Recipe Variations

You could add some cooked bacon crumbles to this dip or even some dried cranberries for a more sweet and savory dip. This dip can also be made in the slow cooker! Add all of the ingredients and turn the slow cooker on low for 2 to 3 hours, stirring a few times.

Cinnamon Pita Fruit Dip

My friends call this "fruit salsa" and it's always a hit!
Kind of a cross between an appetizer and a dessert,
and so refreshing served on a hot day.

15	0	15	10
PREP	COOK	TOTAL	SERVINGS

Ingredients

3 apples of choice

3 kiwi

1 pint strawberries

1 tablespoon lime juice

2 to 3 tablespoons brown sugar
    (depending how sweet you want it)

1 teaspoon ground cinnamon

Cinnamon pita chips or cinnamon
    pretzel crisps for dipping

Directions

1. Dice the apples, kiwi, and strawberries into tiny pieces. Combine into a large bowl.

2. Add lime juice, brown sugar, and cinnamon, toss to coat evenly.

3. Serve with cinnamon pita chips or cinnamon pretzel crisps for dipping.

Helpful Hints

Using a very sharp knife helps tremendously when cutting the fruit. This can be made several hours before serving and stored in a covered container in the fridge until ready to serve. The longer it sits, the fruit will macerate (or produce more liquid) and that's perfectly normal, just stir before serving.

Corn & Black Bean Salsa

This salsa is super easy to make, but it never fails every time you make it. It's always a delicious crowd pleaser! You can even make this the day before and keep it in a covered container in the fridge.

10	0	10	10
PREP	COOK	TOTAL	SERVINGS

Ingredients

2 15 ounce cans corn

1 15 ounce can black beans

1 15 ounce can black eyed peas

2 10 ounce can Rotel Tomatoes

1 4 ounce can green chiles
   or jalapenos

1 red onion (diced)

1 to 1½ cups Italian dressing

1 tablespoon sugar

Kosher salt, pepper

Tortilla chips for dipping

Directions

1. Drain the cans of corn and put the corn into a big bowl.

2. Drain the can of black beans and black eyed peas in a colander and rinse with water. Add the beans to the bowl.

3. Add the Rotel tomatoes, green chilis or jalapenos, and diced red onion to the bowl.

4. Pour the Italian dressing and sugar into the bowl and stir to mix evenly. Add kosher salt and pepper to taste.

5. Serve with tortilla chips for dipping.

Cooking Variations

Might I suggest coating 5 to 6 ears of corn on the cob with olive oil, salt, and pepper. Then grill for 10 minutes, turning a few times. Cut the kernels off for a super fresh version of this salsa! Also, if you have leftovers, this salsa is incredible on grilled chicken that has been marinated in Italian dressing.

Crab & Artichoke Dip

This dip is best served warm or at room temperature. It's extra special in my opinion thanks to the crab and cheesy goodness.

10	25	35	8
PREP	COOK	TOTAL	SERVINGS

Ingredients

8 ounces cream cheese

½ cup sour cream

½ cup mayo

2½ tablespoons Old Bay seasoning

2 tablespoons Worcestershire sauce

2 tablespoons lemon juice

A few dashes of your favorite hot sauce

¼ cup sliced green onions

2 cups shredded Monterey Jack cheese

1 cup shredded parmesan cheese

1 14 ounce can artichoke hearts (drained and chopped)

1 pound canned or fresh crab meat (drain well)

Home Cook Hacks

If serving this with crostini, simply cut a loaf of French bread into slices. Place on a baking sheet, brush the tops with olive oil and season with kosher salt and pepper. Place in a 400 degree oven for 5 minutes and voila... you have crostini!

Directions

1. Put the cream cheese, sour cream, mayo, Old Bay, worcestershire sauce, lemon juice, and hot sauce in a large bowl. Mix with a hand mixer until evenly combined.

2. Add the green onions, both cheeses (save some cheese to add over top), chopped artichokes, and crab to the bowl. Stir until evenly combined with a spoon.

3. Transfer to a cast iron skillet or baking dish, add the remaining cheese over top. Bake in a 400 degree oven for 25 to 30 minutes.

4. Serve with crostini, crackers, or chips.

Roasted Tomato Feta Dip

This is a light, vegetarian dip recipe perfect for summer, but festive enough to serve at any holiday or celebration year round. I love it served with pita chips or torn pieces of Naan bread.

15	40	55	8
PREP	COOK	TOTAL	SERVINGS

Ingredients

5 medium size tomatoes

1 red bell pepper

1 onion

Olive oil, kosher salt, pepper

6 ounces crumbled feta cheese

3 to 4 cloves garlic

2 tablespoons lemon juice

2 tablespoons Italian seasoning

½ to 1 teaspoon crushed red pepper flakes (more or less depending on spice preference)

Pita chips or Naan bread for dipping

Directions

1. Cut the tomatoes in half and squeeze them cut side down in a bowl to get out most of the juice and seeds. Cut the red pepper in half and remove the stem and seeds. Peel the onion and cut into 2 or 3 thick slices.

2. Place the tomatoes, red pepper, and onion on a baking sheet, drizzle both sides with olive oil and season with kosher salt and pepper.

3. Roast in a 425 degree oven for 30 to 40 minutes. Flipping halfway through. Let cool.

Cooking Variations

You can cook this on your smoker or pellet grill set to 225 degrees. Just place the seasoned tomatoes, red pepper, and onion slices on the grill grate for 2 to 2½ hours, flipping halfway through.

4. Put the tomatoes, red pepper, onion, feta, garlic, lemon juice, Italian seasoning, and crushed red pepper flakes in a food processor or blender. Blend on low for at least a minute or until evenly mixed. Taste and add kosher salt and pepper if needed.

5. Refrigerate the dip for several hours and serve with pita chips or Naan bread for dipping.

Roasted Veggie Crostini

This appetizer looks very elegant, but is still fairly simple to make. It stays good in the fridge for a few hours before serving at room temperature.

15	30	45	10
PREP	COOK	TOTAL	SERVINGS

Ingredients

1 red bell pepper

1 yellow bell pepper

1 orange bell pepper

1 red onion

Olive oil, kosher salt, pepper

1 loaf French bread

5 to 8 ounce goat cheese
   or cream cheese

Balsamic glaze

½ cup fresh sliced basil

Home Cook Hacks

Leftovers never go to waste in my house. If you are lucky enough to have some leftover roasted veggies and goat cheese, make them into quesadillas following the recipe on page 77. Be sure to include the balsamic glaze and some basil in the quesadillas

Directions

1. Dice the peppers and onions and place on a baking sheet. Add some olive oil, kosher salt, and pepper and toss until evenly mixed.

2. Roast in the oven at 450 for 20 to 25 minutes and toss several times as they roast. Set aside to cool.

3. Cut the loaf of french bread into slices. Lay them on a baking sheet, brush with olive oil, salt, and pepper just on the top. Bake at 400 for 5 minutes.

4. Spread each slice of bread with goat cheese or cream cheese. Top with the roasted veggies. Drizzle with balsamic glaze and finish with the chopped fresh basil.

Sausage Stuffed Jalapeños

These jalapenos can be served warm or they travel well and serve at room temperature. The ultimate dish to bring for any big game day celebration.

15	35	50	10
PREP	COOK	TOTAL	SERVINGS

Ingredients

15 jalapeno peppers

1 tablespoon olive oil

1 onion (diced)

1 red bell pepper (diced)

4 to 5 cloves garlic (minced)

1 pound ground Italian sausage

Kosher salt, pepper

8 ounces cream cheese

1 ½ cups shredded cheddar cheese

Helpful Hints

You can control the heat level by removing all of the jalapeno seeds for very little heat, or leave some seeds in to add some spiciness to this appetizer. These can also be prepared a day ahead of time and then baked before serving.

Directions

1. Cut the jalapenos in half lengthwise. Using a spoon, scrape out the seeds and ribs. Note: Recommended to wear plastic gloves when handling jalapenos.

2. In a skillet over medium heat add the olive oil, onion, and red pepper. Cook for 5 minutes, stirring occasionally.

3. Add the garlic, sausage, kosher salt, and pepper. Cook 8 to 10 minutes, breaking up the sausage as it cooks.

4. Turn the heat down to low and add the cream cheese. Stir until the cream cheese is melted into the sausage mixture. Turn the heat off and add the cheese, stirring until melted.

5. Fill each jalapeno half with this mixture and place on a lined baking sheet. Bake in a 400 degree oven for 25 minutes.

CHAPTER FOUR

Easy Peasy Weeknight Sides

THERE ARE EXTRA SPECIAL SIDE DISHES TO BRING TO
A PARTY OR HOLIDAY CELEBRATION TO FEED A
CROWD... AND THEN, MY FRIENDS, THERE ARE SIMPLE
SIDES TO SERVE WITH A WEEKNIGHT DINNER.
THAT'S WHAT YOU'LL FIND IN THIS CHAPTER.

SOME SORT OF CARB OR VEGETABLE TO
INCLUDE SOME VARIETY WITH A MAIN DISH,
BUT WITHOUT AFFECTING YOUR SANITY
WAS THE GOAL WITH THESE RECIPES.

Baked Sweet Potato Fries

Homemade fries in the oven are so much healthier than fried. Bonus points that we are using sweet potatoes for some added vitamins. We dip these in ketchup or spicy mayo.

5	25	30	4
PREP	COOK	TOTAL	SERVINGS

Ingredients

1 large sweet potato

2 tablespoons olive oil

½ teaspoon ground cinnamon

½ teaspoon ground cumin

½ teaspoon chili powder

Kosher salt, pepper

Directions

1. Cut the large sweet potato in half, then cut each half into 6 wedges (12 wedges total).

2. Place the sweet potato wedges on a baking sheet. Brush all sides with the olive oil. Sprinkle them with cinnamon, cumin, chili powder, kosher salt and pepper.

3. Bake in a 425 degree oven for 22 to 28 minutes, flip them halfway through.

Cooking Variations

To make these in the air fryer, put the sweet potato wedges in a bowl. Add the olive oil, cinnamon, cumin, chili powder kosher salt, and pepper and toss until coated. Place them in the air fryer basket, set the air fryer to 400 degrees for 16 to 18 minutes.

BBQ Bacon Green Beans

Even though I prefer fresh green beans, sometimes weeknight dinners require simplicity. That's when canned green beans come to the rescue!

10	15	25	4
PREP	COOK	TOTAL	SERVINGS

Ingredients

4 to 5 slices bacon

1 onion (diced)

3 to 4 cloves garlic (minced)

2 15 ounce cans cut green beans (drained very well)

3 tablespoons butter

1 tablespoon BBQ seasoning blend

Kosher salt, pepper

Helpful Hints

To make this even easier, use a teaspoon of garlic powder in place of the fresh minced garlic. Also, a huge time saver for me is using the frozen diced onions to prevent having to cut a fresh onion on busy weeknights.

Directions

1. Set a skillet over medium heat. Use kitchen scissors to cut the bacon into the skillet in bite size pieces. Cook for 5 to 6 minutes, stirring a few times. Drain some of the excess bacon grease.

2. Add the diced onion to the skillet with the bacon, cook for 4 to 5 minutes stirring a few times.

3. Add the garlic, green beans, butter, BBQ seasoning, kosher salt, and pepper. Cook for 4 to 5 minutes, stirring a few times.

4. Taste for seasoning and add more BBQ seasoning, kosher salt, and/or pepper if needed.

Crispy Zucchini Fries

Something magical happens when you use panko bread crumbs! That extra crispy, crunchy coating transforms regular zucchini into one of our favorite side dishes of all time.

10	20	30	4
PREP	COOK	TOTAL	SERVINGS

Ingredients

1 large zucchini (or 2 small zucchini)

2 eggs

1 cup panko breadcrumbs

¼ cup grated parmesan cheese

1 teaspoon garlic powder

Kosher salt, pepper

Nonstick or olive oil cooking spray

Optional: ranch dressing for dipping

Cooking Variations

These can be cooked in the air fryer too! Place the breaded zucchini fries in the air fryer basket and set it to 400 degrees for 14 to 16 minutes.

Directions

1. Cut the zucchini into french fry size wedges.

2. Crack the eggs in a bowl, beat with a fork.

3. Add the panko, parmesan cheese, garlic powder, salt, and pepper into another bowl and stir until evenly mixed.

4. Dip each zucchini fry into the egg, then into the panko mixture, press the panko into the zucchini and place on a baking sheet in a single layer. Repeat with remaining zucchini fries.

5. Spray the fries with the cooking spray and bake in a 400 degree oven for 18 to 22 minutes.

6. Serve with ranch dressing for dipping if desired.

Garlic Parmesan Fingerling Potatoes

You can easily find fingerling potatoes in the produce department of most grocery stores. They are rich and buttery, and some are even purple in color, making for a delicious and easy side dish that seems a little extra special.

5	35	40	4
PREP	COOK	TOTAL	SERVINGS

Ingredients

1½ pounds fingerling potatoes

3 tablespoons melted butter

4 to 5 cloves garlic (minced)

¼ cup grated parmesan cheese

Kosher salt, pepper

Directions

1. Slice the potatoes in half lengthwise and place in a bowl.

2. Pour the melted butter on top of the potatoes and add garlic, parmesan cheese, kosher salt, and pepper. Toss to coat evenly.

3. Place the potatoes on a lined baking sheet. Bake in a 400 degree oven for 30 minutes.

Cooking Variations

This easy side dish can also be cooked in the air fryer. Just put them in the air fryer basket for 15 to 18 minutes at 390 degrees. You can also grill them! Set the grill to medium low, place the potato halves on the grill for 20 to 24 minutes, flipping a few times.

Grilled Corn on the Cob

There's a misconception that in order to grill corn, it must be soaked or the cornsilk removed. That's an extra step I don't always have the energy for. This is my ultimate lazy side dish that's always a hit with my family.

10	10	20	4
PREP	COOK	TOTAL	SERVINGS

Ingredients

4 ears corn on the cob (shucked)
Olive oil, kosher salt, pepper

Directions

1. Brush the corn with olive oil and season all sides with kosher salt and pepper.

2. Preheat the grill to medium heat. Place the corn on the grill grates for 10 to 12 minutes, turning a few times.

Recipe Variations

Although the simplicity of this recipe is all you really need, here are some flavored butters that can be brushed over the corn during the last minute or two on the grill. Melt 3 tablespoons of butter and add...

• Sriracha and a pinch of garlic or garlic powder
• Ground red pepper and a squeeze of honey
• Italian seasoning, garlic powder, and grated parmesan
• Chopped fresh herbs of choice and minced garlic
• Chili powder, paprika, and cumin
• BBQ seasoning blend

Lemon Parmesan Broccoli

Crispy broccoli always wins over mushy broccoli in our family! This flavorful and easy side dish is healthy, delicious, and cooked perfectly to keep it nice and crisp.

5	15	20	4
PREP	COOK	TOTAL	SERVINGS

Ingredients

1 bunch broccoli

1 tablespoon olive oil,
Kosher salt, pepper

2 to 3 lemon wedges

2 to 3 tablespoons grated
parmesan cheese

Cooking Variations

This easy side dish can also be cooked in the air fryer. Place the seasoned broccoli florets in the air fryer basket, set it to 390 degrees for 6 to 8 minutes. Then sprinkle the parmesan cheese over top before serving.

Directions

1. Cut the broccoli into florets, aiming for the same size. Lay the florets on a baking sheet, drizzle the olive oil over top and season with kosher salt and pepper. Toss until evenly coated.

2. Arrange the broccoli on a baking sheet so they are not touching each other to get them nice and crispy, squeeze some lemon juice over top. Place in a 450 degree oven for 10 to 15 minutes, depending on how you like them cooked.

3. Once removed from the oven, sprinkle the parmesan cheese over top and an extra squeeze of lemon if desired.

Skillet Green Beans & Peppers

Fresh green beans and red bell peppers in a skillet along with a simple seasoning may seem boring, but honestly these really bring a mini "wow" factor for an easy weeknight side dish. Best part... no need to boil the green beans first!

10	12	22	6
PREP	COOK	TOTAL	SERVINGS

Ingredients

2 tablespoons olive oil

1 pound fresh green beans (trim ends if needed)

2 red bell peppers (sliced)

Kosher salt, pepper, seasoning blend of choice

4 to 5 cloves garlic (minced)

Recipe Variations

You can mix this side dish up using different seasoning blends such as Old Bay, BBQ, Cajun, and using different steak seasoning blends.

Another way to add more excitement is to top with feta or goat cheese crumbles, and some sliced almonds for some crunch!

Directions

1. Set a large skillet over medium heat. Once hot add the olive oil, green beans, and red bell pepper slices. Season with kosher salt, pepper, and your seasoning blend of choice.

2. Cook the veggies for 8 to 10 minutes, stirring a few times.

3. Add the garlic and cook for another 2 to 3 minutes, or until the vegetables are cooked how you prefer.

4. Taste for seasoning and add more kosher salt, pepper, and/or seasoning blend of choice.

Veggie Fried Rice

This side dish is heavy on the veggies with a little rice.
It's my trick to get the kids to eat their veggies,
thinking they are enjoying fried rice.

5	15	20	4
PREP	COOK	TOTAL	SERVINGS

Ingredients

1 tablespoon vegetable or olive oil

1 8 ounce bag sugar snap peas

1 red bell pepper (sliced)

Kosher salt, pepper

1 cup shredded carrots

3 to 4 cloves garlic (minced)

2 cups cooked Jasmine rice

2 to 4 tablespoons soy sauce

1 egg

Home Cook Hacks

One of my best kitchen hacks is using microwavable rice pouches instead of boiling my own rice. You'll need two pouches of Jasmine rice for this recipe, just cook according to the package directions for rice ready in just minutes!

Directions

1. Set a skillet over medium heat and add the cooking oil, sugar snap peas, red pepper slices, and just a tiny bit of kosher salt and pepper. Stir as this cooks for 3 to 4 minutes.

2. Add the shredded carrots and garlic, cook for another 2 to 3 minutes in the skillet.

3. Add the cooked Jasmine rice and 2 to 3 tablespoons of the soy sauce, cook for another minute. Crack the egg into the rice and veggies, mix around and cook for a few more minutes.

4. Taste for seasoning and add more soy sauce if needed.

CHAPTER FIVE

Side Dishes to Impress a Crowd

NOW THAT WE'VE COVERED THE EASY PEASY SIDES, NOW ONTO THOSE EXTRAORDINARY SUMMER BBQ, PARTY, AND HOLIDAY SIDE DISHES THAT WILL TRULY PROMPT THE QUESTION "HEY, CAN I GET THAT RECIPE?"!

THESE MUST TRAVEL WELL, ABLE TO BE PREPARED AHEAD OF TIME, AND OF COURSE BRING A WOW FACTOR OF DELICIOUSNESS!

BBQ Bacon Slaw

This one was created for a summer BBQ or picnic. It's a nice change from regular coleslaw without too many extra steps. I took help from the store and used coleslaw mix, but you could shred your own veggies if you prefer.

10	10	20	10
PREP	COOK	TOTAL	SERVINGS

Ingredients

1 pound bacon

1 cup mayonnaise

¾ cup BBQ sauce

1 12 ounce bag coleslaw

1 12 ounce bag broccoli slaw

1 bunch green onions (sliced)

Recipe Variations

To spice things up a bit, you could use buffalo sauce in place of the BBQ sauce and add some blue cheese crumbles!

Directions

1. Set a large skillet over medium heat and use kitchen scissors to cut the bacon into bite size pieces right into the skillet. Cook the bacon for 7 to 9 minutes, stirring occasionally.

2. Remove the bacon and place on a plate lined with paper towels.

3. In a small bowl add the mayonnaise and BBQ sauce. Whisk until evenly mixed.

4. Add the coleslaw, broccoli slaw, most of the bacon, and most of the green onions to a large bowl. Add the BBQ dressing and use tongs to mix the slaw until it's evenly combined.

5. Sprinkle the top with remaining bacon bits and green onions. Cover and refrigerate until ready to serve.

Cheesy Corn Casserole

Kind of like cornbread, only creamy and rich! It's also known as corn pudding and highly requested at family or holiday dinners!

10	45	55	10
PREP	COOK	TOTAL	SERVINGS

Ingredients

1 15 ounce box honey cornbread mix

2 eggs

1 15 ounce can corn (drained)

1 15 ounce can creamed corn

1 stick melted butter

½ cup sour cream

2 cups shredded cheddar cheese

Directions

1. Put the cornbread mix, eggs, corn, creamed corn, melted butter, and sour cream in a bowl and stir until evenly combined. Add the cheese and fold the cheese in until evenly mixed.

2. Pour this mixture in a greased 9×13 casserole dish. Bake at 350 degrees for 45 to 50 minutes.

Recipe Variations

You can add a 4 ounce can of diced green chiles or jalapenos to the mix for some added spice. Also, you could use pepper jack or any other cheese of choice to add your own spin.

Candied Brussel Sprouts

Some people turn their noses up at brussel sprouts, but these are not your typical brussels. Lots of amazing flavors and textures in this extra special side dish.

5	25	30	8
PREP	COOK	TOTAL	SERVINGS

Ingredients

6 to 8 slices bacon

1 onion (diced)

1 apple (diced)

2 tablespoons butter

1½ pounds brussel sprouts (cut in half lengthwise)

1 cup chicken broth

3 tablespoons brown sugar

½ cup dried cranberries

Kosher salt, pepper

Optional toppings: crumbled goat cheese, candied pecans

Directions

1. Use kitchen scissors to cut the bacon into bite size pieces directly into a large skillet over medium heat. Cook for 5 to 6 minutes, remove the bacon pieces from the pan and set aside, leaving the bacon grease in the skillet.

2. Add the onions to the skillet with bacon grease over medium heat. Cook for 3 to 5 minutes and set aside.

3. Into the same skillet add the apples. Cook for 3 to 5 minutes and set aside.

Helpful Hints

I love making this dish in my 12 inch cast iron skillet. It helps caramelize the brussel sprouts perfectly. Also, I recommend a granny smith apple both for the firm texture and tart flavor. If bringing this side dish to another location, simply transfer to a casserole dish or foil pan. Cover and warm in the oven before serving.

4. Add butter to the same large skillet, still over medium heat. When the butter is melted, place the brussel sprouts cut side down in the skillet. Cook for 4 minutes, then add the chicken broth and brown sugar. Cook for 4 more minutes, gently stirring the mixture, but keeping the brussel sprouts cut side down.

5. Flip brussel sprouts over and add the bacon, onions, apples, dried cranberries, kosher salt, and pepper. Stir together and cook for 1 more minute. Taste for seasoning, add more kosher salt and pepper if needed.

6. Serve with goat cheese and candied pecans over top if desired.

Cheesy Scalloped Potatoes

A giant pan of cheesy potato yumminess is always a popular side dish at any party or celebration. These are extra rich and decadent thanks to the heavy cream!

15	90	115	10
PREP	COOK	TOTAL	SERVINGS

Ingredients

2 tablespoons olive oil

1 onion (diced)

4 to 6 cloves garlic (minced)

Kosher salt, pepper

4 Russet potatoes (skin on, sliced very thin, mine were ⅛ ½ inch)

1 pound sliced cheese of choice (American, cheddar, gruyere, gouda)

1 to 1½ cups heavy cream

1 to 2 cups shredded cheese of choice

Helpful Hints

If you have a manolin, use it to create extra thin and even slices of potatoes. Or at least use a good, quality sharp knife. The presentation looks great in a cast iron skillet, but a foil casserole dish will allow for the easiest cleanup.

Directions

1. Set a skillet over medium heat (I used a 12 inch cast iron skillet and baked the scalloped potatoes in the same skillet). Add a tablespoon of the olive oil and the diced onion. Cook for 3 to 4 minutes, stirring a few times.

2. Add the minced garlic, kosher salt, and pepper and cook 2 to 3 more minutes. Remove from the skillet and set aside.

3. Add the remaining tablespoon of olive oil to the skillet and brush evenly over the skillet (or a 9x13 casserole dish if not baking in the cast iron) and up the sides to prevent sticking.

4. Place a layer of the thinly sliced potatoes in the skillet or casserole dish, kosher salt and pepper, a layer of cheese slices, and onions. Repeat the layers a few times.

5. Carefully pour the heavy cream over the potatoes, use just enough to barely cover the potatoes.

6. Set the oven to 350 degrees and cook the potatoes 1 hour and 15 minutes to 1½ hours. Sprinkle the shredded cheese over top during the last 15 to 20 minutes of cooking.

Green Bean Casserole

This, my friends, is NOT your traditional Thanksgiving green bean casserole. It's unbelievably tasty, decadent, and fresh!

5	60	65	10
PREP	COOK	TOTAL	SERVINGS

Ingredients

3 pounds fresh green beans (trimmed and cut in half)

4 tablespoons butter

16 ounces baby portobello mushrooms (sliced)

1 onion (diced)

4 to 6 cloves garlic (minced)

Kosher salt, pepper

2 teaspoons Old Bay seasoning

1 pint heavy cream

1 tablespoon fresh thyme leaves

6 ounces grated parmesan cheese

4 cups cubed French or Italian bread (½ inch cubes)

Directions

1. Fill a large pot with water and bring to a boil. Add 2 tablespoons of the kosher salt and the green beans. Once it comes back to a boil, cook for 7 minutes, drain and set aside.

2. In the same pot over medium heat, add 2 tablespoons of the butter, mushrooms, onions, and garlic. Season with kosher salt, pepper and Old Bay. Cook for 7 to 8 minutes, stirring occasionally.

3. Add the heavy cream and 1/2 of the thyme leaves. Raise the heat to high, bring to a boil, and reduce to medium low and simmer for 8 to 10 minutes. Stir in 4 oz of the grated parmesan cheese and green beans.

4. Let this cook for a few minutes and taste for seasoning and add more kosher salt, pepper and/or Old Bay if needed. Pour this mixture in a greased 9×13 pan.

5. Put the cubes of bread in a large mixing bowl. Melt the remaining 2 tablespoons butter and add to the bowl of bread cubes along with remaining parmesan cheese and thyme leaves. Add kosher salt and pepper to taste and toss until evenly coated.

6. Put the bread cubes over top of the green bean and mushroom casserole, pressing the bread cubes into the casserole.

7. Bake in a 400 degree oven for 35 to 45 minutes.

Helpful Hints

If the sauce is too thin when removing the casserole from the oven, bake for an additional 5 to 10 minutes. The heavy cream may need more time to thicken, especially if the oven door keeps being opened and closed while it cooks, as happens a lot on holidays. You may also need to press the bread cubes into the casserole a few more times.

Grilled Corn & Bacon Salad

This light and fresh salad screams summer! Make a few hours ahead and store in the fridge until ready to serve.

10	10	20	10
PREP	COOK	TOTAL	SERVINGS

Ingredients

1 pound bacon

10 to 12 ears corn on the cob

1 red bell pepper

1 red onion (peeled and cut in thick slices)

4 tablespoons olive oil

Kosher salt, pepper

4 tablespoons lime juice

2 tablespoons sugar

1 cup chopped, fresh cilantro

Directions

1. Set a skillet over medium heat and use kitchen scissors to cut the bacon right into the skillet in bite size pieces. Cook for 7 to 9 minutes, stirring occasionally. Remove from the pan, put on a plate lined with paper towels, and set aside.

2. Put the corn, red bell pepper, and thick red onion slices on a tray. Brush all sides with 2 tablespoons of the olive oil and sprinkle all sides with kosher salt and pepper.

3. In a small bowl add the remaining 2 tablespoons olive oil, lime juice, sugar, and more kosher salt and pepper. Stir until evenly mixed and set aside.

Recipe Variations

Add jalapenos or poblano peppers for some extra flavor. Just season and grill the same as the other veggies. The addition of crumbled feta cheese and/or sliced cherry tomatoes would also add something special. Feel free to use fresh basil in place of the cilantro if preferred.

4. Preheat the grill to medium high. Add the corn, red pepper, and onion slices on the grill for 10 to 12 minutes, turning a few times throughout.

5. Let them cool slightly and cut the kernels off the corn, remove the seeds and stems from the peppers and dice, and dice the onion.

6. Put into a large bowl and add the bacon, cilantro, and lime dressing. Stir until evenly mixed. Taste for seasoning and add more kosher salt, pepper, olive oil, and/or lime juice if needed.

Recipe Variations

You can easily use a pound of your favorite pasta of choice, if desired, in place of the tortellini. Other additions such as sliced banana pepper rings, sun dried tomatoes, sliced marinated artichokes, fresh parmesan cheese, and/or olives make this dish extra yummy and unique.

Italian Tortellini Pasta Salad

This is not your typical, boring pasta salad!
Easy to make most of it ahead of time and store in the
fridge until ready to serve. This one does NOT last long.

15	3	18	10
PREP	COOK	TOTAL	SERVINGS

Ingredients

1 20 ounce bag frozen cheese tortellini

20 slices pepperoni

15 slices salami

8 slices deli ham

8 slices provolone cheese

¾ cup mayonnaise
   (maybe a bit more)

¾ cup Italian dressing
   (maybe a bit more)

2 tablespoons Italian seasoning

Kosher salt, pepper

1 pint grape or cherry tomatoes

1 cup shredded iceberg lettuce

Directions

1. Boil the tortellini according to the package directions (mine boiled in salted water for 3 minutes). Drain and rinse with cold water.

2. Cut the pepperoni in half, and cut the salami, ham, and provolone cheese into smaller pieces.

3. Put the cold tortellini in a bowl and add the pepperoni, salami, ham, cheese, mayo, Italian dressing, Italian seasoning, kosher salt, and pepper. Toss until combined and store covered in the fridge until ready to serve.

4. When ready to serve, add the tomatoes and lettuce. Stir until combined and add more mayo and Italian dressing if needed. Serve right away.

Stovetop Macaroni & Cheese

This is by far the easiest way I have made mac and cheese, with just a few simple ingredients. A great holiday worthy side dish for sure!

10	40	50	10
PREP	COOK	TOTAL	SERVINGS

Ingredients

1 pound elbow macaroni
 (or short cut pasta of choice)
1 quart heavy cream
Kosher salt, pepper
12 ounce block Colby Jack cheese
½ cup shredded parmesan cheese

Helpful Hints

If you are bringing this dish to another location, simply transfer it to a 9x13 casserole dish or foil pan. Sprinkle more cheese over top if desired. Warm in the oven before serving.

Directions

1. Boil the elbow macaroni in a large pot according to package directions. Save a half cup of the starchy pasta water and set aside. Pour the macaroni into a pasta strainer and rinse very well with cold water so it doesn't become mushy.

2. Set the same large pot over high heat and add the quart of heavy cream, kosher salt, and pepper. Bring to a boil, watching carefully as it will bubble up (if bubbles too much remove from heat for a moment).

3. Once boiling, reduce the heat to medium low and cook for 30 minutes, stirring several times and scraping the sides a few times.

4. Use a
box grater to
shred the cheese.
Once the cream has
cooked for 30 minutes
it should be reduced by
half. Add the cooked pasta,
shredded Colby jack cheese and
parmesan cheese, stir until melted.

5. Add 1/4 cup of the reserved pasta water
and stir until combined. Taste for seasoning and add
more kosher salt and pepper as needed. Add more of the
reserved pasta water if you prefer a creamier mac and cheese.

CHAPTER SIX

Stupid Simple Dinners

HOME COOKS NEED RECIPE HACKS AND A FEW GO-TO EASY MEALS, AM I RIGHT?! THIS MEANS USING SOME STORE BOUGHT INGREDIENTS, SHORTCUTS, AND KID FRIENDLY RECIPE MODIFICATIONS.

SOME OF THESE ARE LITERALLY SO EASY, YOU MIGHT WONDER WHY IN THE WORLD THEY EVEN NEED A WRITTEN RECIPE.

WELL, FRIENDS, I'M HERE TO GIVE YOU ALLLLLL THE DINNER IDEAS (NO MATTER HOW SIMPLE) IN ONE PLACE THAT YOU CAN CHOOSE FROM ON THOSE NIGHTS WHEN YOU DON'T FEEL LIKE COOKING.

Asian Steak Bites

A few minutes to cut the steak and a few minutes in the skillet and dinner is done. I like to serve this with rice and broccoli for a complete meal. This is another great one to marinate the night before to cook up quickly on the night you make it.

10	5	15	4
PREP	COOK	TOTAL	SERVINGS

Ingredients

1½ pounds flat iron steak
(or sirloin or strip steak)

2 tablespoons soy sauce

1 tablespoon honey

4 to 5 cloves garlic (minced)

Kosher salt, pepper

Olive oil

Optional: store bought yum yum sauce, green onions, sesame seeds

Directions

1. Cut the steak into 1 inch cubes and place in a gallon size plastic bag. Add the soy sauce, honey, garlic, kosher salt, and pepper (just a small amount of kosher salt is needed). Toss until evenly coated. Cover and refrigerate for a few hours or overnight.

2. Set a large skillet over medium heat. Add some olive oil and the steak bites. Cook for 5 to 8 minutes, stirring a few times.

3. Serve with the Yum Yum sauce for dipping. Garnish with sesame seeds and green onions if desired.

Home Cook Hacks

You can easily use a teriyaki sauce for the marinade in place of the homemade marinade in this recipe to make it even easier... store bought marinades can be a home cook's best friend! If serving with rice, might I suggest the microwave Jasmine rice pouches. So good mixed together with the steak, yum yum sauce, and rice for the perfect bite.

Baked Lemonade Chicken Thighs

The kids are instantly sold on this dish because it has "lemonade" in the title. It's also a fun, finger licking good dinner that's also budget friendly. Marinate the night before to make this dish super quick on a busy night.

15	45	60	4
PREP	COOK	TOTAL	SERVINGS

Ingredients

5 pounds chicken thighs
(bone in, skin on)

¼ cup lemon juice

¼ cup brown sugar

2 tablespoons Dijon mustard

1 tablespoon olive oil

1 tablespoon lemon zest

1 tablespoon Worcestershire sauce

5 to 6 cloves garlic

Kosher salt, pepper

3 tablespoons butter
(cut into smaller pieces)

Optional: lemon wedges

Recipe Variations

You can use any bone in cut of chicken for this dish like drumsticks or whole chicken wings. In place of the lemon feel free to add BBQ seasoning to mix it up a little.

Directions

1. Trim any extra skin from the chicken thighs if needed and place them in a gallon size plastic bag.

2. Add the lemon juice, brown sugar, Dijon mustard, olive oil, lemon zest, Worcestershire sauce, garlic, kosher salt, and pepper to the bag. Massage the bag until combined. Marinate in the fridge for several hours.

3. Place the chicken thighs in a casserole dish. Add the butter and sprinkle a little extra kosher salt and pepper over top.

4. Bake in a 375 degree oven for 40 to 50 minutes, or until the internal temperature is above 165 degrees.

5. Spoon some of the lemon butter sauce in the casserole dish over the chicken when serving and with extra lemon wedges to squeeze over top if desired.

Baked Chicken Pesto Quesadillas

This is another recipe that uses the meal prep chicken on page 87. So it literally takes 10 minutes to throw together and the oven does the rest. This eliminates the long, slow process of making one... quesadilla... at... a... time... in a skillet.

10	10	20	4
PREP	COOK	TOTAL	SERVINGS

Ingredients

8 soft taco size flour tortillas

Olive oil

3 to 4 cups shredded mozzarella cheese

2 cups cooked, shredded chicken

6 to 8 ounces store bought pesto

Pizza sauce for dipping

Recipe Variations

Once you have perfected this easy baked method for making super quick quesadillas, try these flavor mash-ups . . .
(continued on next page)

Directions

1. Lay the tortillas flat and brush each with the olive oil.

2. Lay 4 of the tortillas on a lined baking sheet (or 2 baking sheets depending on size), oil side down.

3. Put some shredded mozzarella on each tortilla, add the cooked, shredded chicken, and spoonfuls of the pesto. Then add more cheese and top with the remaining tortillas, oil side up.

4. Bake in a 400 degree oven for 10 to 12 minutes, or until the tortillas are crisped and golden brown to your liking.

5. Cut the quesadillas into smaller triangles and serve with pizza sauce for dipping.

Recipe Variations

• Swap out the pesto for buffalo sauce or
BBQ sauce and dip them in ranch dressing
• Add ingredients such as banana peppers,
sun dried tomato slices, and/or
jarred artichoke hearts
• Swap out the mozzarella for cheddar cheese,
replace the pesto with bacon, and dip in ranch
for a great chicken bacon ranch version
• Use pepperoni in place of the chicken,
or any favorite pizza toppings,
to create a delicious pizza-dilla
• Up the "fancy" level and
play around with adding
different cheeses such as
goat cheese, asiago,
fresh mozzarella,
and/or feta cheese.

Baked Pork Tenderloin with Apples

Pork and apples are a perfect combo, so why not make a one pan meal with both?! So simple, will have your kitchen smelling incredible, and that first bite is sure to bring a smile to everyone!

5	40	45	4
PREP	COOK	TOTAL	SERVINGS

Ingredients

1 onion

2 apples (I used Honeycrisp)

1 tablespoon olive oil

½ teaspoon ground cinnamon

Kosher salt, pepper

1 pork tenderloin

¼ cup hoisin sauce

2 tablespoons pure maple syrup

Cooking Variations

This recipe can also be made in the slow cooker! Just arrange the onion, apples, and pork in the slow cooker, mix the remaining ingredients together in a bowl, pour over top, and set the slow cooker to low for 6 hours.

Directions

1. Dice the onion and slice the apples (about 1½ inch slices). Put the onion and apples in a 9×13 casserole dish or sheet pan.

2. Add the olive oil, cinnamon, kosher salt, and pepper. Toss until evenly coated. Make room for the pork tenderloin and place in the middle of the pan.

3. In a small bowl whisk together the hoisin sauce and maple syrup. Brush this mixture on all sides of the pork tenderloin. Sprinkle the pork with kosher salt and pepper.

4. Place in a 400 degree oven for 30 to 40 minutes (until internal temp is 145 degrees). Toss the apples and onions halfway through cooking.

Crispy Baked Parmesan Chicken

A 5 ingredient kid friendly dinner sounds almost too good to be true. This one I assure you can be whipped up in no time on even the busiest weeknight.

10	15	25	4
PREP	COOK	TOTAL	SERVINGS

Ingredients

½ cup mayonnaise

½ cup grated parmesan cheese

4 to 5 cloves garlic (minced)

Kosher salt, pepper

4 thin cut chicken breasts

¼ cup panko bread crumbs

Cooking Variations

This dish can easily be made in your air fryer! Place the chicken in the air fryer basket set to 400 degrees for about 12 to 14 minutes.

Directions

1. Put the mayonnaise, parmesan, garlic, kosher salt, and pepper in a bowl and whisk until evenly mixed.

2. Put the thin cut chicken breasts on a lined baking sheet. Spread the garlic parmesan sauce over each one. Top each chicken with the panko bread crumbs (press the panko slightly into the sauce).

3. Bake in a 400 degree oven for 15 to 18 minutes, turn the broiler on high during the last two minutes to crisp the top.

Note: Thicker chicken breasts may take longer, make sure the chicken is above 165 degrees before serving.

One Pan Salmon & Potatoes

This recipe has a creole mustard sauce, but has many flavor variations to make this dinner over and over without getting bored. Gotta love a one pan, easy dinner with hardly any cleanup!

5	40	45	4
PREP	COOK	TOTAL	SERVINGS

Ingredients

1 pound redskin potatoes

Olive oil, kosher salt, pepper

½ cup mayonnaise

½ cup whole grain or Dijon mustard

1 tablespoon Cajun seasoning

2 pound side of salmon (skin on)

½ cup panko breadcrumbs

Directions

1. Dice the potatoes and spread evenly on a lined baking sheet, drizzle with olive oil and sprinkle kosher salt, and pepper over top. Toss to coat evenly. Place the baking sheet in a 400 degree oven for 20 to 25 minutes, toss them halfway through cooking time.

2. Mix the mayonnaise, mustard, and Cajun seasoning together in a small bowl

Recipe Variations

Feel free to use another side of your favorite fish, including trout, catfish, or halibut. Also try these sauce flavors in place of the mustard and Cajun seasoning. Just mix ½ cup mayonnaise together with the following and use the same directions as above...

- ½ cup BBQ sauce and 1 tablespoon BBQ seasoning blend
- ½ cup teriyaki sauce and 1 tablespoon minced garlic
- ½ cup grated parmesan cheese and 1 tablespoon Italian seasoning
- ½ cup sweet chili sauce and 1 tablespoon Sriracha

3. Remove the baking sheet from the oven. Add 2 tablespoons of the mustard sauce to the potatoes, toss until evenly coated and make room in the center of the pan for the salmon.

4. Place the salmon in the center of the baking sheet, season with kosher salt and pepper. Spread another 2 to 3 tablespoons of the mustard sauce on the salmon. Press the panko bread crumbs on top of the salmon

5. Place the baking sheet back into the 400 degree oven for 14 to 18 minutes. Turn the broiler on high for an additional 2 minutes to crisp the panko bread crumbs. Serve with the remaining mustard sauce.

Home Cook Hacks

The leftovers for this dish are even better the next day, so make more and plan ahead to enjoy the leftovers for lunch! Or give the leftovers a makeover and serve in quesadillas with added cheese. Or on sub buns as a sausage and pepper sandwich with melted mozzarella cheese and pizza sauce.

Roasted Sausage & Veggies

Another one pan wonder of a meal! Mix it up and make it your own by adding or swapping out different veggies such as mushroom halves, yellow squash, sliced carrots, and/or cherry or grape tomatoes.

10	40	50	4
PREP	COOK	TOTAL	SERVINGS

Ingredients

1 pound smoked sausage (chicken, pork, or turkey sausage, any flavor)

1 red bell pepper

1 yellow bell pepper

1 red onion

1 zucchini

2 tablespoons olive oil

1 tablespoon balsamic vinegar

4 to 5 cloves garlic (minced)

1 tablespoon Italian seasoning

Kosher salt, pepper, crushed red pepper flakes

Optional: crumbled feta or goat cheese

Directions

1. Cut the smoked sausage, red pepper, yellow pepper, red onion, and zucchini into 1 to 2 inch pieces. Place on a lined baking sheet.

2. Add the olive oil, balsamic vinegar, garlic, Italian seasoning, kosher salt, pepper, and crushed red pepper flakes. Toss until evenly coated. Add more kosher salt and pepper over top if needed.

3. Place the baking sheet in a 425 degree oven for 35 to 40 minutes, toss the sausage and veggies halfway through cooking.

4. Serve with crumbled feta or goat cheese if desired.

Shrimp Garlic Ramen Noodles

There's something comforting and familiar about ramen noodles. This recipe creates a stir fried ramen that's ready in minutes!

10	10	20	4
PREP	COOK	TOTAL	SERVINGS

Ingredients

3 packages ramen noodles
  (any flavor)

2 tablespoons vegetable or olive oil

1 pound jumbo shrimp
  (peeled and deveined)

Kosher salt, pepper

1 onion (diced)

6 to 7 cloves garlic (minced)

2 to 3 tablespoons teriyaki sauce

2 tablespoons soy sauce

3 tablespoons butter

2 eggs

½ cup green onions (sliced)

Directions

1. Boil the noodles according to package directions (throw away flavor packet), drain and rinse very well with cold water.

2. Set a large skillet or wok over medium high heat. Add some of the oil and the shrimp. Season with kosher salt and pepper, cook 3 to 4 minutes and remove from the skillet.

3. Add a little more oil and the onion, cook for a minute or two.

4. Add the garlic and cook for about 45 seconds and then add the cooked noodles, teriyaki sauce, soy sauce, butter, and eggs.

Recipe Variations

You can mix this same recipe up by using different store bought sauces in place of the teriyaki sauce... might I suggest hoisin sauce, stir fry sauce, or Pad Thai sauce?! Jazz it up even more with toppings such as crushed peanuts, sesame seeds, and sriracha! And you can certainly use cooked chicken or steak in place of the shrimp.

5. Cook the noodles for 5 to 6 minutes, stirring and mixing everything together. Press noodles into the skillet or wok with a spatula to create crispy parts of the noodles if desired.

6. Add the cooked shrimp and green onions and cook for 1 to 2 more minutes.

Simple Shredded Meal Prep Chicken

You'll find a few recipes in this book that require "cooked, shredded chicken". You can shred up a store bought rotisserie chicken, or make a big batch of this healthy, budget friendly, meal prep chicken that tastes MUCH better than store bought.

5	40	45	8
PREP	COOK	TOTAL	SERVINGS

Ingredients

3 to 4 chicken breasts
Olive oil, kosher salt, pepper

Optional: crushed red pepper flakes, seasoning blend of choice

Recipe Variations

In addition to the recipes in this book that call for shredded chicken, use in quesadillas, nachos, wraps, or use the chicken to top salads. It's also a great, healthy snack to have on hand in the fridge.

Directions

1. Place the chicken in a casserole dish.

2. Drizzle with olive oil and season with kosher salt, pepper, crushed red pepper flakes, and/or seasoning blend of choice.

3. Place in a 375 degree oven for 30 to 40 minutes.

4. Let cool, shred with your hands, and store in a covered container in the fridge for up to 4 days.

Steak with Italian Cream Sauce

Throw some steak on the grill (or skillet) and whip up a homemade cream sauce in no time... I pinky promise the cream sauce is super simple.

10	25	35	4
PREP	COOK	TOTAL	SERVINGS

Ingredients

4 tablespoons butter

½ cup beef or chicken broth

1½ cups heavy cream

1 tablespoon Dijon mustard

1 tablespoon Italian seasoning

Kosher salt, pepper

4 New York Strip steaks
(or steak of choice)

Recipe Variations

You can add so many flavors to the cream sauce to make it unique and different every time you make this meal. Might I suggest fresh minced garlic, blended chipotle peppers in adobo for a spicy version, some pesto, or swap out the Italian seasoning for some fresh chopped herbs like thyme, chives, or rosemary.

Directions

1. Set a saucepan over high heat and add the butter, broth, heavy cream, Dijon mustard, Italian seasoning, kosher salt, and pepper.

2. Bring this to a boil and reduce the heat to medium low, simmer for 14 to 16 minutes. Let the sauce come to room temp while you grill the steaks, it will get thicker as it sits.

Note: Watch carefully when bringing to a boil, if it starts to bubble over remove from heat for a moment.

3. Season the steaks with kosher salt and pepper. Preheat the grill to medium high heat (or a large skillet with some olive oil). Grill the steaks 3 to 5 minutes per side depending on thickness and how you prefer them cooked.

4. Serve the steaks with the cream sauce.

CHAPTER SEVEN

Company Worthy Dinners

WHEN HAVING FRIENDS AND FAMILY OVER, RECIPES THAT ARE A LITTLE MORE SHOW STOPPING ARE A MUST. I LIKE TO MAKE RECIPES THAT CAN BE PREPARED AHEAD OF TIME WHEN ENTERTAINING GUESTS, SO I HAVE INCLUDED TIPS AND TRICKS TO DO AS MUCH AS POSSIBLE BEFORE THEY ARRIVE.

SOME OF THESE ARE ALSO PERFECT TO SEND TO FRIENDS AND FAMILY WHO ARE SICK OR NEED A LITTLE EXTRA LOVE SENT THEIR WAY. OF COURSE YOU DON'T HAVE TO WAIT FOR COMPANY, THESE CAN BE DINNER ANY NIGHT YOU HAVE A LITTLE EXTRA TIME.

Baked Tortellini with Sausage

This comfort food dish is a one pan wonder that's perfect to make ahead of time, just store it in the fridge and bake right before serving. Also great to bring dinner to a friend, just prepare the dish and give them the baking instructions.

15	40	55	8
PREP	COOK	TOTAL	SERVINGS

Ingredients

1 36 ounce bag frozen cheese tortellini

2 to 3 tablespoons olive oil

1 pound smoked sausage (sliced)

3 cups fresh, chopped spinach

8 ounces baby portobello mushrooms (sliced)

Kosher salt, pepper

2 tablespoons butter

1 pint heavy cream

4 ounces pesto

1 cup shredded parmesan cheese

1 cup shredded mozzarella cheese

Directions

1. Cook the tortellini in salted, boiling water according to package directions in a large soup pot. Drain them in a colander and rinse well with cold water to prevent them from becoming mushy.

2. Set the same large pot over medium high heat, add some olive oil and the sliced smoked sausage. Cook 3 to 4 minutes or until browned how you prefer and set them aside.

Recipe Variations

You can easily swap out the sausage for chicken or shrimp if your family prefers. And also leave out the spinach and mushrooms for picky eaters. In a time pinch, you can use a 16 ounce jar of alfredo sauce in place of adding the butter and heavy cream.

3. Add the spinach and mushrooms, kosher salt, and pepper to the same pot. Cook for 5 to 6 minutes, stirring a few times. Remove and set aside with the sausage.

4. Rinse out the same pot with water and set it back on the stove on high. Add the butter, heavy cream, kosher salt, and pepper. Once that comes to a boil, reduce the heat to medium low and simmer for 5 to 6 minutes. Add the pesto and parmesan and cook 2 to 3 more minutes, stirring a few times.

5. Add the cooked tortellini, sausage, spinach, and mushrooms to the pot with the pesto cream sauce and gently stir until evenly mixed. Pour into a 9×13 casserole dish. Top with the mozzarella cheese and bake in a 350 degree oven for 15 to 20 minutes.

Baked Ziti with Burrata Cheese

This is one giant pan of pure cheesy comfort food!
The burrata makes this dish extra decadent and creamy.
You can make this ahead of time and bake when you'd like.

15	30	45	8
PREP	COOK	TOTAL	SERVINGS

Ingredients

1 pound ziti pasta

1 pound ground Italian sausage

1 onion (diced)

6 to 8 cloves garlic (minced)

1 32 ounce jar pasta/
    marinara sauce

½ cup red wine (or chicken
    or beef broth)

1 tablespoon Italian seasoning

Kosher salt, pepper

2 8 ounce containers
    burrata cheese

2 cups shredded mozzarella
    or Italian blend cheese

Optional: fresh basil to garnish

Directions

1. Cook the ziti pasta according to package directions. Drain and rinse with cold water, set aside.

2. Set the same pot that you cooked the pasta in over medium heat. Add the Italian sausage, cook for 5 to 6 minutes, breaking it apart as it cooks.

3. Add the diced onion and cook for 4 to 5 minutes with the sausage. Add the garlic and cook for 1 more minute.

4. Put the cooked ziti into the pot along with the pasta sauce, red wine (or broth), Italian seasoning, kosher salt, and pepper. Cook for 2 minutes, stirring until evenly combined.

5. Pour half of this mixture in a 9×13 casserole dish. Drain the liquid in the containers of burrata and add half of the burrata cheese by tearing the balls into smaller pieces and sprinkle half of the shredded mozzarella cheese.

6. Pour the remaining ziti mixture over top and top with remaining burrata cheese and mozzarella cheese. Bake in a 375 degree oven for 20 to 25 minutes.

7. Turn the broiler on high for a minute or two if you would like a golden brown cheese. Garnish with fresh basil if desired.

Helpful Hints

If you cannot find burrata cheese, you can substitute fresh mozzarella cheese. If you'd like to add some spice to this dish, add some crushed red pepper flakes with the kosher salt and pepper.

Chicken Broccoli Crêpes

Homemade crepes are so easy to make and quite impressive.
This is one that travels well if you're bringing it to another house.

15	40	55	6
PREP	COOK	TOTAL	SERVINGS

Ingredients

3 eggs

¾ cup flour

¾ cup water

Kosher salt, pepper, olive oil

1½ cups cooked, shredded chicken

1½ cups cooked, chopped broccoli

1 16 ounce jar alfredo sauce

2 cups shredded cheddar cheese

¾ tablespoon Old Bay seasoning
(or seasoning blend of choice)

¼ cup milk or water

Helpful Hints

This should make 6 crepes total, the batter makes slightly more but leaves room for error if you accidently make the first crepe too thick. Remember the crepes should be pretty thin.

Directions

1. Crack the eggs in a bowl and add the flour, water, kosher salt, and pepper. Whisk until combined and let sit for 10 minutes.

2. Set a medium sized skillet over medium low heat. Add some olive oil and a spoonful or so of the crepe mixture, turn the skillet in a circle motion so the crepe spreads out evenly and is thin. Cook about a minute per side, remove, and repeat making the remaining crepes adding more olive oil each time.

3. While the crepes cool, make the filling by combining the chicken, broccoli, half of the alfredo sauce, half of the cheese, and Old Bay or seasoning blend of choice (and kosher salt and pepper if needed).

4. Put some of the chicken broccoli filling down the center of each crepe, then roll them up and place in a greased 9x13 baking dish.

5. Add the milk or water to the alfredo sauce jar, shake, and pour over top. Sprinkle the remaining cheese over top. Bake in a 375 degree oven for 22 to 27 minutes.

Chicken Cordon Bleu Casserole

So creamy, decadent, and delicious! It also uses the Meal Prep Chicken recipe on page 87. If bringing this dish to a friend or family member, just prepare it up until baking and send over the cooking directions.

10	20	30	8
PREP	COOK	TOTAL	SERVINGS

Ingredients

4 cups cooked, shredded chicken

½ pound deli sliced ham (diced)

8 ounces sliced Swiss cheese (diced)

1 10.5 ounce can cream of chicken soup

1 8 ounce container sour cream

½ cup Dijon mustard

Kosher salt, pepper

45 buttery crackers (I used Ritz)

2 tablespoons melted butter

Home Cook Hacks

I am a huge fan of the easy salad kits at the store to serve with this dinner. If you are already entertaining, take help from the store and mix up a salad kit for a complete meal. Also, for easy cleanup use a foil disposable pan.

Directions

1. Put the chicken, diced ham, diced cheese, cream of chicken soup, sour cream, Dijon mustard, kosher salt, and pepper in a bowl. Toss until evenly mixed and put this into a greased 9×13 casserole dish.

2. Put the crackers in a gallon size plastic bag and crush them (I used a rolling pin). Pour the melted butter in the bag and shake until evenly coated. Put the crackers in an even layer over the casserole.

3. Bake in a 400 degree oven for 20 to 25 minutes.

Loaded Buffalo Chicken & Potatoes

Another all in one complete meal, but this one is not so much fancy and more on the casual side. All the ingredients are familiar and loved by most people.

10	45	55	6
PREP	COOK	TOTAL	SERVINGS

Ingredients

2 pounds redskin potatoes

Olive oil, kosher salt, pepper

2 pounds boneless, skinless chicken thighs (or breasts)

1 packet dry ranch seasoning

½ to ¾ cup buffalo wing sauce

2 cups shredded cheddar cheese

8 to 10 slices bacon (cooked and crumbled)

Optional toppings: ranch dressing, sour cream, green onions

Recipe Variations

You could turn this dish into a BBQ party on a sheet pan by substituting the buffalo sauce for your favorite BBQ sauce. Add some spice by using pepper jack cheese in place of the cheddar and some sliced jalapenos.

Directions

1. Cut the potatoes into bite size pieces and place them on a large baking sheet. Drizzle the potatoes with olive oil, season with kosher salt and pepper, and toss until evenly mixed.

2. Bake the potatoes in a 425 degree oven for 15 to 20 minutes. While the potatoes are baking, cut the chicken thighs or breasts into bite sized pieces.

3. Remove the baking sheet with the potatoes and carefully add the chicken, dry ranch seasoning, kosher salt and pepper, and more olive oil if needed. Use tongs to toss everything together until it's evenly mixed.

4. Place the chicken and potatoes back into the 425 degree oven for 25 to 30 minutes, use tongs to toss them once or twice.

5. Once the chicken and potatoes are cooked, add the buffalo sauce and toss together. Sprinkle the cheese and bacon over top and place back into the oven for 5 more minutes or until the cheese is melted.

6. Serve with optional toppings such as ranch dressing, sour cream and/or green onions.

Oven Roasted Shrimp "Boil"

One of the absolute best meals to share with loved ones is a giant shrimp boil! But this one is baked, instead of boiled, for extra flavor. Dig in, get messy, and enjoy! The recipe can easily be doubled if feeding a crowd.

10	30	40	4
PREP	COOK	TOTAL	SERVINGS

Ingredients

1 pound petite red potatoes

1 to 2 pounds jumbo shrimp (deveined, shells on)

1 pound smoked andouille sausage

4 ears corn on the cob (shucked)

2 tablespoons olive oil

1 to 2 tablespoons lemon juice

1 tablespoon Old Bay seasoning (plus more to sprinkle over top)

Home Cook Hacks

Serve family style over newspaper lining the center of the table if desired. Also with sauces such as store bought remoulade sauce, seafood sauce, and/ or melted garlic butter for dipping. You could also mix together a cup of mayo and add some lemon juice, Old Bay, and hot sauce for an easy homemade sauce.

Directions

1. Boil the red potatoes in salted water for 7 to 8 minutes. Let them cool slightly and cut them in half.

2. Pat the shrimp dry with paper towels. Cut the smoked sausage into 1 inch pieces. Cut each ear of corn into 3 pieces.

3. Put the potatoes, shrimp, sausage, and corn on a baking sheet along with the olive oil, lemon juice, and Old Bay seasoning. Toss until evenly coated. Sprinkle with a little more Old Bay over top.

4. Place the baking sheet into a 425 degree oven for 20 minutes.

Optional: Turn the broiler on high for the last 2 minutes to make everything more golden brown if desired.

Sausage & Kale Soup

Soup is so fun to make in my opinion.
And this one is extra warm and comforting on a cold day.

10	30	40	8
PREP	COOK	TOTAL	SERVINGS

Ingredients

1 pound ground Italian sausage

1 tablespoon olive oil

1 onion (diced)

2 red bell peppers (diced)

Kosher salt, pepper,
  crushed red pepper flakes

5 to 7 cloves garlic (minced)

4 cups chicken broth

1 28 ounce can crushed tomatoes

1 15 ounce can cannellini beans
  (drained and rinsed)

1 tablespoon Italian seasoning

5 cups chopped kale

1 cup heavy cream

Recipe Variations

You could use ground Italian turkey or chicken sausage and half and half in place of the cream to lighten this recipe up a bit. Also feel free to use chopped spinach in place of the kale. If you don't like spicy, leave out the crushed red pepper flakes.

Directions

1. In a large soup pot over medium heat, add the ground Italian sausage. Cook 5 to 7 minutes, breaking it apart as it cooks. Drain excess grease and set the sausage aside.

2. To the same pot, add olive oil, diced onion, diced red bell pepper, kosher salt, pepper, and crushed red pepper flakes. Cook over medium heat for 5 to 7 minutes, stirring occasionally. Add the garlic, cook for 1 minute, then add the chicken broth.

3. Add the cooked sausage, tomatoes, cannellini beans, Italian seasoning, kale, more kosher salt, and pepper. Bring to a boil, reduce heat to simmer for 10 to 15 minutes.

4. Add the heavy cream, bring to a boil and simmer for 5 more minutes. Taste for seasoning and add more kosher salt, pepper, and crushed red pepper flakes if needed.

Shrimp & Grits

This is one of my all time favorite recipes! A classic recipe that is certainly a splurge meal, but worth every calorie 🙂

10	40	50	6
PREP	COOK	TOTAL	SERVINGS

Ingredients

Cheesy Grits

3 cups chicken broth

¾ cup corn grits or polenta

1 cup heavy cream

2 tablespoons butter

Kosher salt, pepper

1 cup shredded cheddar cheese

Shrimp and Cream Sauce

2 tablespoons olive oil

1 pound jumbo shrimp
  (peeled and deveined)

Old Bay seasoning

1 onion (diced)

4 to 6 cloves garlic (minced)

1 cup heavy cream

¾ cup chicken broth

Lemon wedges, parsley for garnish

Directions

Cheesy Grits

1. Put the chicken broth in a large saucepan or pot. Bring to a boil and add the grits, heavy cream, butter, kosher salt, and pepper.

2. Reduce the heat to medium low and cook for 30 minutes, stirring several times.

3. Stir in the cheddar cheese and remove from heat. If not creamy enough, stir in more heavy cream or broth. Taste for seasoning and add more kosher salt and pepper if needed.

Shrimp and Cream Sauce

1. Set a skillet over medium heat, once hot add the olive oil and shrimp. Season the shrimp with Old Bay and cook 1 to 2 minutes per side. Remove from the skillet and set aside.

2. Add the onion and more Old Bay to the same skillet over medium heat, add more olive oil if needed. Cook for 3 to 4 minutes, add the garlic and cook for another minute.

3. Add the heavy cream and chicken broth to the skillet. Once simmering/ bubbling, reduce heat to medium low and simmer for 5 to 6 minutes, stirring a few times. Taste for seasoning and add more Old Bay if needed.

Recipe Variations

Cook some diced andouille sausage in the skillet after the shrimp for a few minutes, remove from the skillet, and top the shrimp and grits with the sausage for some extra flavor! You could also use buffalo sauce in place of the chicken broth for the cream sauce for a spicy version.

Spinach Ricotta Chicken Meatballs

These meatballs can be served by themselves, maybe with a side of garlic bread. Or you can use them to make meatball subs or top them on a plate of pasta. The ricotta cheese is the secret ingredient that makes a very light and airy meatball!

10	45	55	8
PREP	COOK	TOTAL	SERVINGS

Ingredients

1 tablespoons olive oil

1 onion (diced)

6 ounces fresh spinach leaves (chopped)

Kosher salt, pepper, crushed red pepper flakes

Italian seasoning

1 pound ground chicken

½ cup breadcrumbs

5 to 6 cloves garlic (minced)

1 egg

¾ cup ricotta cheese

1 to 2 cups marinara sauce

1 cup shredded mozzarella cheese

Directions

1. Set a skillet over medium heat and add the olive oil and diced onion. Cook for 3 to 4 minutes. Add the chopped spinach, kosher salt, pepper, crushed red pepper flakes, and Italian seasoning. Cook 3 to 4 more minutes stirring a few times.

2. While this cools, put the chicken, bread crumbs, garlic, egg, ricotta cheese, kosher salt, pepper, crushed red pepper flakes, and Italian seasoning in a bowl. Once the spinach mixture is cool add it to the bowl.

3. Mix together with your hands until evenly combined. Roll 8 meatballs with your hands and place in a casserole dish.

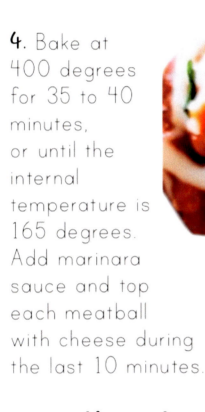

4. Bake at 400 degrees for 35 to 40 minutes, or until the internal temperature is 165 degrees. Add marinara sauce and top each meatball with cheese during the last 10 minutes.

Home Cook Hacks

You can make these meatballs in any size, for example you may want to make them smaller for meatball subs and decrease the cook time by about 10 minutes. You can make a big batch of the meatballs and freeze them for up to 3 months, just do not add the marinara sauce and cheese until after cooking.

Tex Mex Style Lasagna

Guests usually expect a lasagna, but you could really wow them with this version of a classic! Serve with chips and salsa on the side in place of the traditional garlic bread.

15	60	75	8
PREP	COOK	TOTAL	SERVINGS

Ingredients

1 pound ground beef

1 packet taco seasoning

Nonstick cooking spray

2 12 ounce cans green enchilada sauce

8 to 10 soft taco size tortillas (corn or flour, cut in half)

1 15 ounce can corn (drained)

4 cups shredded cheddar or Mexican blend cheese

Optional toppings: sour cream, cilantro, lime wedges, hot sauce

Directions

1. Cook the ground beef according to the directions on the taco seasoning packet. Let the meat come to room temperature.

2. Spray the bottom and sides of a 9×13 casserole dish with nonstick cooking spray. Add a few spoonfuls of the green enchilada sauce and spread evenly.

3. Place 4 tortilla halves flat in the dish, cut side toward the outer edges of the pan. Arrange so they are in a single layer (it is ok if there are a few small spaces or gaps, or use additional tortilla pieces to fill gaps if needed).

Home Cook Hacks

If serving this to guests, set up a topping bar so everyone can add their own. This will make your job a little easier as the host and eliminate the passing of toppings around the table.

4. In an even layer sprinkle 1/3 of the cooked taco meat and corn, and 1/4 of the enchilada sauce and cheese. Add another layer of tortillas. Repeat 2 more layers of filling and tortillas. Top with 1 more tortilla layer. Spread the remaining enchilada sauce and cheese.

5. Spray a piece of foil with more non-stick cooking spray, cover the lasagna with the foil, oil side down. (This will prevent the cheese from sticking). Bake in a 375 degree oven for 45 minutes.

6. Remove the foil and bake for an additional 15 minutes. Serve with sour cream, cilantro, fresh lime wedges to squeeze over top, and/or hot sauce is desired.

CHAPTER EIGHT

"Gotta Have One More Bite" Desserts

I ONLY DO "EASY" DESSERTS. I AM NOT
A LOVER OF BAKING, BUT MORE A
LOVER OF ENJOYING SIMPLE DESSERTS
THAT DON'T REQUIRE TOO MUCH WORK.

SO HERE ARE MY EASIEST, BUT
TOTALLY ADDICTING AND DELICIOUS,
SWEET TREATS.

Caramel Bread Pudding

Bread pudding is my dessert weakness! This one has a homemade salted caramel sauce that's incredible!

15	60	75	10
PREP	COOK	TOTAL	SERVINGS

Ingredients

2 sticks butter

1 cup brown sugar

½ cup sugar

½ tablespoon kosher salt

1 quart half and half

4 eggs

1 teaspoon vanilla extract

1 18 ounce loaf Brioche bread (cut into small cubes)

Optional toppings: whipped cream, bottle of caramel sauce, fresh fruit

Recipe Variations

You could also use the sweet Hawaiian rolls in place of the Brioche if desired. Also, for a little extra fun and flavor add 2 tablespoons of dark rum or bourbon to the bread mixture.

Directions

1. In a small saucepan over medium to medium high heat add butter, brown sugar, and sugar. Whisk slowly for 5 to 6 minutes until it's golden brown, lower heat to medium or medium low after it starts bubbling. Add the kosher salt and set aside to cool slightly.

2. While the caramel cools, put the half and half, eggs, and vanilla extract, in a large bowl and whisk until combined. Add the pieces of Brioche bread and most of the caramel sauce and fold together.

3. Put this mixture into a greased 9×13 casserole dish, drizzle remaining caramel sauce over top. Let this sit while the oven preheats.

4. Place in a 350 degree oven for 1 hour to 1 hour 15 minutes.

5. Serve with whipped cream, more caramel drizzled over top, and with fresh fruit if desired.

Chocolate Lava Cake

This dessert is perfect for an evening at home because it makes 4 servings and is best served warm right out of the oven.

10	15	25	4
PREP	COOK	TOTAL	SERVINGS

Ingredients

4 ounces dark chocolate

1 stick butter

1½ cups powdered sugar

½ cup flour

3 eggs

1 teaspoon vanilla

Nonstick cooking spray

Optional: more powdered sugar, vanilla ice cream

Cooking Variations

These can easily be cooked in your air fryer instead of the oven. Place the ramekins or glass bowls in the air fryer basket and set it to 400 degrees for 12 to 14 minutes.

Directions

1. Put the chocolate and butter in a large to medium size bowl. Microwave for 1 minute, stir until the butter and chocolate are melted and combined.

2. Add the powdered sugar, flour, 2 of the eggs plus just the yolk from the third egg, and the vanilla. Stir until combined.

3. Spray 4 ramekins or small oven safe glass bowls with nonstick spray. Divide the batter evenly between the 4 bowls.

4. Place the bowls on a baking sheet and place in the oven at 400 degrees for 12 to 14 minutes. Let them cool for a few minutes then carefully turn them upside down on a plate (use a towel as the bowls will be hot).

5. Leave them upside down on the plates for a few minutes, then carefully remove the bowls. Sprinkle more powdered sugar over top and serve with vanilla ice cream if desired.

Churro Caramel Cake

Since I'm not a baker, this cake uses a box mix to make it as easy as possible. The cinnamon sugar topping on the cake is incredible.

10	35	45	10
PREP	COOK	TOTAL	SERVINGS

Ingredients

Cake

1 15 ounce box yellow cake mix

4 eggs

1 stick melted butter

1 cup milk

1 teaspoon ground cinnamon

Churro Caramel Topping

⅓ cup sugar

⅓ cup brown sugar

1 teaspoon ground cinnamon

1 tablespoon melted butter

3 to 4 ounces caramel sauce

Directions

Cake

1. Put the cake mix in a large bowl and add the eggs, melted butter, milk, and cinnamon.

Note: These ingredients are different from the package directions.

2. Using a hand mixer, mix the batter for 2 minutes.

3. Pour the batter into a greased 9×13 pan. Bake in a 350 degree oven for 32 to 36 minutes.

Home Cook Hacks

Most home cooks take a little help from store bought ingredients. By adding an extra egg, using butter in place of vegetable oil, and substituting milk for the water that a box cake usually calls for brings a homemade or bakery taste to regular box cake.

Churro Caramel Topping

1. Mix the sugar, brown sugar, and cinnamon together in a small bowl.

2. While the cake is still warm, brush the melted butter over top and sprinkle half of the cinnamon sugar mix.

3. Drizzle the caramel over top and wait until the caramel melts, it will become an even layer after a few minutes.

4. Sprinkle the other half of the cinnamon sugar mixture and serve.

Easy No Churn Ice Cream

Rich and decadent homemade ice cream that requires no fancy equipment or ice cream machine! Get the kiddos involved with this one, SO fun to make this as a family and play around with different flavors.

5	0	8hr	8
PREP	COOK	TOTAL	SERVINGS

Ingredients

1 pint heavy cream (very cold)

1 14 ounce can sweetened condensed milk

2 teaspoons vanilla

1 to 2 cups chopped candy, fruit, or flavor additions of choice

Directions

1. Put the cold heavy cream in a bowl. Beat with a hand mixer on medium speed for 3 to 4 minutes.

2. Add the sweetened condensed milk, vanilla, and candy, fruit, or additions of choice. Gently fold together until combined.

3. Transfer to a freezer safe container, cover, and place in the freezer for at least 8 hours.

4. When ready to scoop, leave the ice cream on the counter for several minutes to soften slightly.

Recipe Variations

Flavor combos for this basic ice cream recipe are endless, just a few ideas but not limited to...

- Crushed pineapple and maraschino cherries
- Sliced peaches, strawberries, or berries
- Chocolate chips, toffee or peanut butter chips
- Peanut butter, hot fudge, or caramel sauce
- Chopped cookies, brownies, or candy bars
- Salty snacks like chopped pretzels or nuts

Ice Cream Cone Pie

A perfect summer dessert! All the yumminess of an ice cream cone but made into a frozen pie.

15	0	5hr	8
PREP	COOK	TOTAL	SERVINGS

Ingredients

12 sugar cones

2 tablespoons sugar

6 tablespoons melted butter

1 quart vanilla ice cream (or flavor of choice)

1 7 ounce bottle chocolate magic shell

Optional: chopped peanuts

Helpful Hints

If chocolate magic shell won't shake or seems thick, place in a cup with hot water for a few minutes so it drizzles nice and thin. Also, I recommend sitting this out on the counter for at least 15 minutes before slicing.

Directions

1. Put the sugar cones in a food processor or blender. Pulse a few times. Add the sugar and melted butter and pulse a few more times.

2. Put this mixture into a pie pan and use a cup or spoon to help form into a pie crust, flat on the bottom and up the sides of the pie pan. Place in the freezer for at least 3 hours.

3. Let the ice cream come to room temp (I set mine out for 45 minutes) and put in the pie crust. Use a spoon to flatten the top.

4. Drizzle the magic shell over top and sprinkle the chopped peanuts over top.

5. Place back in the freezer for at least 2 hours before serving.

Mini Oreo Cheesecakes

Remember how I said these are all EASY desserts... well this one uses a box of no bake cheesecake mix to ensure I kept my promise :)

15	0	2hr	12
PREP	COOK	TOTAL	SERVINGS

Ingredients

14 Oreo cookies (plus a few more to crumble over top)

4 tablespoons melted butter

1 box no bake cheesecake mix (plus additional ingredients on the package directions)

Recipe Variations

You can really use any cookie in place of the Oreos to create cheesecakes with different flavors. You'll need about 1½ cups total of cookie crumbs. These would be great with chocolate chip, peanut butter, or Biscoff cookies!

Directions

1. Put the cookies and butter into a food processor, pulse until they become crumbs. If you don't have a food processor, crush them in a gallon size plastic baggie.

2. Put the cookie crumbs into a muffin tin (makes 12 total) and press them into the bottom. You can use a small cup or spoon for this.

3. Make the no bake cheesecake mix according to the package directions. Divide the cheesecake evenly into the muffin tin. Use the back of a spoon to flatten the top slightly.

4. Place in the freezer for at least 2 hours. Turn the muffin tin upside down to easily remove them. Crumble a few Oreo cookies on top to decorate.

Pumpkin Cheesecake Balls

Little bites of heaven dipped in white chocolate could not get any easier to make! The kids love helping me make these.

15	0	15	18
PREP	COOK	TOTAL	SERVINGS

Ingredients

1 14 ounce loaf pumpkin bread
   (store bought or made from a mix)
8 ounces cream cheese
   (at room temperature)
20 ounces white chocolate chips

Recipe Variations

Not a pumpkin fan? No problem! You can use a lemon pound cake, chocolate pound cake, or even your favorite muffins in place of the pumpkin bread.

Directions

1. Put the pumpkin bread in a large mixing bowl. Using a hand mixer on low, carefully break up the pumpkin bread into crumbs. Remove 1/4 cup of the pumpkin breadcrumbs to use to sprinkle over top later.

2. Add the cream cheese and blend with the hand mixer for 1 minute, it will be lumpy.

3. Roll this mixture into 18 cake balls and place on a baking sheet or tray. Freeze for 20 minutes.

4. Pour the white chocolate chips into a microwave safe bowl. Microwave on high for 1 minute, stir the chips and microwave 10 more seconds. If they are not melted, microwave for 10 seconds at a time and stir until they are melted.

5. Drop a pumpkin cake ball into the melted chocolate and using a fork, evenly coat in chocolate and place on a lined baking sheet or tray. Sprinkle some of the reserved pumpkin bread crumbles on top. Repeat with remaining cake balls.

Salted Caramel Pretzel Bark

This recipe is probably the most involved of all the dessert recipes here, but WELL worth it! This dessert is legendary in my family.

10	10	20	8
PREP	COOK	TOTAL	SERVINGS

Ingredients

Nonstick cooking spray

1 bag pretzels
   (enough to cover a baking sheet)

2 sticks butter

1 cup brown sugar

12 ounce bag semi-sweet
   chocolate chips

Kosher salt or sea salt

Directions

1. Line a baking sheet with foil, cover well with nonstick spray, and lay pretzels in a single layer (use smaller pretzel pieces to fill in empty spaces. Preheat the oven to 350 degrees.

2. In a small saucepan over medium heat add butter and brown sugar. Whisk slowly for 4 to 6 minutes until it's golden brown and bubbly.

3. Pour caramel mixture over pretzels and put in the oven for 5 minutes.

4. Sprinkle chocolate chips over the bubbling caramel pretzels. Put back in the oven for 2 minutes. Using a rubber spatula spread the melty chocolate evenly. Sprinkle the kosher or sea salt over top.

5. Put the baking sheet in the freezer for at least a half hour. Break the pretzel bark into bite size pieces. Store in the fridge, covered.

Helpful Hints

As the caramel is coming to a boil, keep whisking slowly and don't leave the stove as it could boil over. Lower heat to medium low if needed. When you pour the caramel over top of the pretzels, it may not cover all of the pretzels, but will bubble and even out as it cooks in the oven.

STAY CONNECTED

 Cooks Well With Others
If You Give A Girl A Grill
KAT TEGS Designs

 @cooks_well_with_others
@ifyougiveagirlagrill
@kattegsdesigns

 @cookswellwithothers
@ifyougiveagirlagrill
@kattegsdesigns

 @cookswellwithothers
@ifyougiveagirlagrill
@kattegsdesigns

 @_cwwo
@iygaag
@kattegsdesigns

 @cookswellwithothers

ABOUT THE AUTHOR

I'm Cheri and I am a self taught home cook here to share my recipes with you and some of my home cook hacks and helpful hints. I am a mother of four incredible kids, wife to an amazing husband, former second grade teacher, and current food blogger. I share my recipes on my websites CooksWellWithOthers.com and IfYouGiveAGirlAGrill.com! Come visit my websites for even more recipes in addition to the recipes in this book.

I was so excited to collaborate on this cookbook with my daughter, Kat, who did an incredible job on the design, graphics, and just making it gorgeous. You can see more of her work at her website KatTegsDesigns.com!

Kat Tegenkamp is a self taught graphic designer with a passion for creating art. You can find her illustrated books and journals available on Amazon. As well as apparel and sticker designs available on kattegsdesigns redbubble shop and website.

Made in United States
Orlando, FL
07 June 2025

61920730R00074